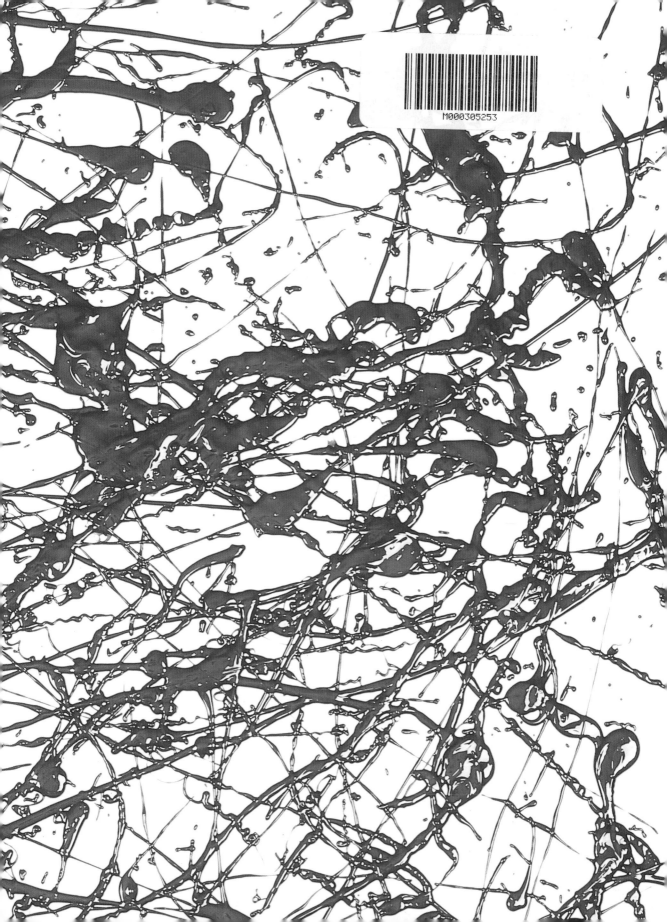

MASTERING
CHOCOLATE

Ltd.

MARK TILLING

First published in April 2017 by B. Dutton Publishing Limited, The Grange, Hones Yard, Farnham, Surrey, GU9 8BB, UK. Copyright: Mark Tilling 2017

ISBN-13: 978-1-905113-56-9

Publisher: Beverley Dutton

Editor-in-Chief: Jenny Weaver

Creative Director: Sarah Ryan

Commissioning Editor: Jennifer Kelly

Copy Editors: Adele Duthie, Emily Gussin and Frankie New

Home Economists: Shirley Quarmby and Claire Russell

Photography: Rob Goves

Chocolate supplied by Callebaut™

Printed and bound in Slovenia by arrangement with Associated Agencies Limited, Oxford

ACKNOWLEDGEMENTS

I would like to thank a few people: if it wasn't for their help over the years and while writing this book, I couldn't have done it.

First I would like to thank my wife, Vicky. She's my best friend and has stood by me for many years and throughout the process of writing this book. I love you lots xx

Thanks to Beverley and Robert Dutton for giving me the opportunity to write another book and for their support over the last eight years that I have been working at Squires Kitchen.

To Sarah Ryan for designing such an amazing-looking book: it's always a pleasure working with you. Jenny Weaver for keeping me on track with the writing of this book: you've been a great support, thank you. Thanks also to Jen Kelly, Frankie New, Adele Duthie and Emily Gussin: you guys rock.

To everyone at Callebaut, especially Beverley Dunkley and Julie Sharp, thanks for all your support over the years.

Thanks to Rob Goves for the photography. It's always great working with you, you do a fantastic job every time.

To Shirley Quarmby and Claire Russell: your input has been invaluable, thank you.

Thanks to Andrea Saunders and Jan Hill, housekeepers at Squires Kitchen International School, for all their help with cleaning up after the photoshoots – one of the most important jobs!

Thank you to Claire Clark for her kind words in the foreword – she's a world-renowned pastry chef so it was a privilege to showcase my work to her in *Bake Off: Crème de la Crème*.

Last but not least, thank you to Helen Vass and Samantha Rain for being such great sports and agreeing to coming on *Bake Off: Crème de la Crème* with me. We make a great team, friends for life.

MASTERING
CHOCOLATE

Recipes, tips and
techniques from
the award-winning
master chocolatier

FOREWORD

I first became aware of the amazing, multi-talented Mark Tilling in 2006 when he won the UK Chocolate Masters. Mark went on to win the title a second time in 2008: he certainly managed to grab my attention and admiration, and we quickly became friends.

Mark's accolades are many: double gold medals for his chocolate work, too many silver medals to mention and a CV which includes an impressive list of Michelin-starred restaurants and hotels. It's not surprising then that Mark was quickly snapped up by Callebaut™ to be their UK Chocolate Ambassador.

I haven't met a more gentle and kind man in our industry, and Mark has remained approachable and humble throughout his success. He is an inspiration to his students at Squires Kitchen International School in Farnham, Surrey, where he can be found inventing and creating the most magnificent pâtisserie and confectionery delights. Never one to rest on his laurels, Mark is constantly reinventing and progressing.

Our paths crossed once again when Mark led a team of talented pastry chefs to compete with 14 other teams on BBC Two's *Bake Off: Crème de la Crème*. Mark, Helen and Samantha stunned the home viewer with their lavish and beautifully handcrafted pâtisserie creations. They whipped up sculptures of the Lake District and massive towers of toppling kitchen implements from chocolate in mere hours without even breaking a sweat, impressing myself and the other judges and leaving no doubt as to who would scoop the title.

Mastering Chocolate presents a whole host of dazzling, mind-blowing culinary techniques including hot chocolate truffles – oh yes, it is possible. The recipes are easy to follow and understandable: Mark's step-by-step pictures make otherwise difficult professional techniques achievable even for novices, plus there are lots of helpful tips. I am personally looking forward to trying out the chocolate, maple and bacon macaroons, a flavour combination I came to adore whilst working in the States.

Pastry chefs and chocolate fans of all levels will love this book. It's crammed full of fun, tasty sweet treats which you can't fail to enjoy making, and of course eating. *Mastering Chocolate* deserves to have pride of place in every chocolate lover's kitchen.

Claire Clark MBE, MOGB

INTRODUCTION

I love chocolate. There are so many different ways you can use it and things you can create – truffles, desserts, pastries, showpieces, entremets, tiered wedding cakes. I wanted *Mastering Chocolate* to be colourful and fresh, and to showcase and celebrate chocolate in all its diversity.

I also love teaching and enjoy passing on my skills; it's my great pleasure to share some of my favourite recipes with you in this book. I've developed them throughout my career, from winning the UK Chocolate Masters to becoming Head Tutor at Squires Kitchen International School.

When I read a cookery book, I like to see lots of pictures – not just of the finished dish, but of the process so it really helps you to learn. That's why I have included photographs of each step of the way for all of the recipes to help you get the right results.

Some recipes in this book might look daunting but they really are simple when you break them down: just take your time and follow the steps. You'll be amazed at what you can achieve!

Mark Tilling

CONTENTS

BITE-SIZE

INDIVIDUAL

CUT & SHARE

SHOWSTOPPERS

MASTERING
CHOCOLATE

AUTHOR PROFILE

Mark Tilling has been working as a pâtissier and chocolatier for over 25 years. He credits his passion for pastry to his family, saying, 'I remember from a very early age watching both my grandmothers making sweet things… I always knew I wanted to work in this area.'

While completing a BTEC First Diploma in Hotel and Catering Studies and an NVQ Level 3 in Professional Cookery: Patisserie and Confectionery at Southampton City College, Mark's first job was working in the pastry kitchen of a local hotel at the weekends. His favourite memories of working there centre around the lavish New Year's Eve buffets: 'We could really go to town with them and make all kinds of pastries.' It was here at the age of 16 that Mark met chef Martin Nash, who would have a huge influence on his life and career over the years.

Mark went on to work in many hotels and restaurants including The Lanesborough in London, Lainston House Hotel in Winchester, Hotel du Vin in both Winchester and Bristol, and Le Pavé d'Auge in Normandy, France, which boasts a Michelin star. He has received many awards for his chocolate and pâtisserie work, including numerous gold and silver medals for his desserts and petits fours, and double gold for his chocolate showpieces. Mark won two UK Chocolate Masters competitions in a row in 2006 and 2008, going on to represent the UK at the finals of the World Chocolate Masters in 2007 and 2009. In the later competition he came 7th in the world, which at the time was the UK's highest ever placing.

Following these accomplishments, Mark was made a UK Callebaut™ Chocolate Ambassador as well as Head Tutor of Squires Kitchen International School in Farnham, Surrey. He says, 'I have a great passion for teaching and enjoy passing on my skills to other people.' He is a regular contributor to *Cakes & Sugarcraft* magazine and has written a number of books on chocolate and pâtisserie.

Along with former Squires Kitchen International School students and fellow pastry chefs Helen Vass and Samantha Rain, Mark won the first series of BBC2's *Bake Off: Crème de la Crème* in April 2016, beating 14 other professional teams to be crowned Britain's best team of pastry chefs.

AWARDS AND ACHIEVEMENTS

CACAO BARRY
WORLD CHOCOLATE MASTERS

2006: Winner of the UK Chocolate Masters

2006

2007

2007: 12th in the World Chocolate Masters Final, Paris

2008

2008: Winner of the UK Chocolate Masters

2009: Became a UK Callebaut™ Chocolate Ambassador

2009

2009: 7th in the World Chocolate Masters Final, Paris

Joined Squires Kitchen International School as Resident Tutor

2010

2009: Showpiece displayed in the front window of Harrods, London

2010: Launch of first book, *Squires Kitchen's Guide to Working with Chocolate* (B. Dutton Publishing)

Made the 200th Anniversary Baddeley Cake

2011

2013: Chocolate dress shown at Salon du Chocolat, London

2012

2013

2011: Launch of second book, *Squires Kitchen's Guide to Making Macaroons* (B. Dutton Publishing)

2014: Chocolate dress displayed at Harvey Nichols, London, and the Salon du Chocolat, London

2014

2014: Launch of *The Art of Sugarcraft* (B. Dutton Publishing), a collaborative book by Squires Kitchen tutors, winner of the Best UK Food Book for Professionals in the 2014 Gourmand World Cookbook Awards

2015

2015: Became Head Tutor of Squires Kitchen International School

2016

2016: Winner of BBC Two's *Bake Off: Crème de la Crème*

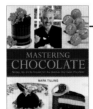

2017: Launch of *Mastering Chocolate* (B. Dutton Publishing)

2017

FROM
BEAN TO BAR
THE CHOCOLATE JOURNEY

I love chocolate because it's so versatile; you can combine it with pretty much any ingredient and it transforms the flavours. I'm really interested in the history and I also find the process fascinating; there's a great deal of work that goes into the development from bean to bar.

I visited cocoa plantations in Brazil in 2011 and Ghana in 2012 to meet the farmers and find out as much as I could about how cocoa beans are grown and transformed into chocolate; this was as part of my role as UK Chocolate Ambassador for Callebaut™ and much of the information that follows was provided by them, with thanks. I took the photographs on these pages during both of those trips.

CULTIVATING THE COCOA BEAN

The cocoa tree, *Theobroma cacao*, grows in in the warm and humid area in a narrow belt just 10° north and 10° south of the equator. The scientific name for the tree's genus, *Theobroma*, is derived from the Greek for 'food of the gods'. This evergreen tree can reach up to 8m (26ft) tall and requires a humid climate, regular rainfall and good soil as well as a shady location. Young trees thrive in tropical temperatures within the protective shadow of tall-growing plants such as banana plants or palm trees.

Cocoa trees originate from Central and South America's rainforests but today cocoa is cultivated globally in carefully grown plantations in the tropical rainforests of Africa, Asia and Latin America. The largest cocoa-producing countries are Ivory Coast, Ghana and Indonesia. Today, Africa is the main overall cocoa supplier, with 75% of the world's cocoa crop. For the small farms in tens of thousands of African villages, cocoa cultivation represents an important source of income.

From around the fifth or sixth year of their lives, the trees begin to bear pods and start to play their full economic role in the many plantations. This is limited to 25 years, after which it is time to replace them with younger trees.

The three main varieties of the cocoa tree are Criollo, Forastero and Trinitario. The descendants that we see in the plantations today are usually cultivated or coincidental hybrids of these varieties, each with their own particular characteristics.

CRIOLLO   FORASTERO   TRINITARIO

Criollo, also known as the prince among cocoa trees, produces pods with a very thin peel. The cocoa itself has a very pale colour and a unique refined aroma. This variety produces small harvests and is also very fragile.

Forastero is a stronger type of tree that is easier to cultivate and produces larger yields. The cocoa pods have a thicker peel and a coarser, stronger aroma. Cocoa from the Forastero beans is often called bulk cocoa because it gives chocolate a typical recognizable basic aroma. This cocoa therefore forms the basic ingredient in most chocolates and can often account for 80% of the cocoa mixture.

Trinitario is a cross between the former types of trees and has characteristics of both: it has a strong but relatively refined aroma and, moreover, is very easy to cultivate.

The cocoa tree flowers in two cycles of six months each year. Hundreds of tiny, pinkish-white, five-petalled flowers grow in clusters on the trunk and branches. Only a few will be fertilised, naturally by midges or by hand, and usually no more than 40 develop into cocoa pods. These resemble elongated, green melons.

After six months the cocoa pods are fully grown and have changed colour from green to yellow-orange. Taking care not to damage the branches, the plantation workers harvest the pods by cutting through the stalk with a sharp blade. This takes place twice a year; in most African countries such as Ivory Coast, the main harvest lasts

from October to March and the interim harvest from May to August.

The cocoa pods are left to ripen for seven to 10 days after the harvest, then the outer peel is opened using long knives and a very precise cutting movement, without touching the beans. The pulp containing the precious cocoa beans is removed from the pods and collected in large baskets.

The beans are then, depending on the variety, left to ferment for five to seven days on the ground or in trays, covered with banana leaves. The important fermentation process removes any of the remaining fruit pulp that sticks to the beans. The beans change colour from beige to purple and develop their aroma.

After fermentation, the cocoa beans are spread out and left to dry in the sun for about six days. The beans are turned regularly so that they retain approximately 3% of their moisture content. Drying is essential, both for stopping the fermentation process and for storage. After drying, the beans are graded and packed into hessian sacks for delivery to the chocolate manufacturer.

FROM BEAN TO LIQUOR

When they arrive, the cocoa beans are first cleaned of any stones, dirt and sand and quickly dried under heaters. This makes it easier to crush the beans and to remove the shell around them. Only the pieces of kernel or 'nibs' remain.

The cocoa nibs are then roasted, which develops their characteristic aromas. The blend of cocoa beans from the different regions will determine the characteristic flavour of each chocolate.

The nibs are put into grinders and are first ground coarsely, then to a super-fine cocoa liquor (pure cocoa mass). The heat created by this process melts the cocoa butter present in the liquor, turning the cocoa liquor to liquid.

The cocoa liquor is now ready for use as an ingredient of chocolate. It can also be further processed into cocoa powder and cocoa butter.

FROM LIQUOR TO COCOA POWDER AND COCOA BUTTER

Cocoa liquor is made up of two different components – cocoa butter and cocoa powder – which are both essential for several different applications.

These two components can only be separated by pressing the liquid cocoa liquor through a very fine sieve. Usually, it is poured into cylindrical tubes and compressed under high pressure. The cocoa butter that is fine enough to pass through a microscopically fine sieve is collected while the cocoa solids remain pressed together in the cylinder, resembling a flattened cake.

At the end of the pressing procedure, this 'cake' is removed and ground further in different stages into a very fine cocoa powder.

FROM LIQUOR AND COCOA BUTTER TO CHOCOLATE

Cocoa liquor, cocoa butter, sugar, powdered milk and vanilla are the raw materials with which manufacturers such as Barry Callebaut make all of the different types of chocolate.

Dark chocolate is made with cocoa liquor, cocoa butter and sugar.

For **milk chocolate**, milk powder is added.

White chocolate is made with cocoa butter, sugar and milk powder (no cocoa liquor, which explains the ivory colour of white chocolate).

Natural vanilla can be added to all kinds of chocolate to enhance the taste.

The ingredients are first weighed very precisely for the particular type of chocolate that is about to be produced. They are then mixed together and blended into a chocolate dough. This mixture is pressed between rollers to form a fine powder: this will give the finished chocolate a smooth texture and a homogenous flavour. If the average size of the particles in this chocolate powder is smaller than the distance between the taste buds on your tongue – so small you will never physically feel them – it will be a smooth chocolate, free from any grainy texture.

This chocolate powder is kneaded for hours until the aromas have fully developed in 'conches', large tanks with powerful stirring equipment inside which slowly kneads the mixture. Due to the friction caused by the stirring, heat develops. This heat melts the powder into a homogeneous paste and causes the unpleasant, acidic aromas to evaporate.

At the end of the conching process, cocoa butter is added to make the chocolate liquid, as well as soya lecithin to stabilise the liquidity and emulsify the chocolate. The liquid chocolate is now stored in large, heated tanks so that it can be further processed into blocks, callets (drops) or other solid shapes.

TAKING SHAPE

The liquid chocolate must first be tempered so it can eventually harden. Tempering ensures the correct formation of the cocoa butter crystals so that the chocolate will harden into shiny, hard and solid shapes.

Only when it has been tempered can the chocolate be poured into moulds or deposited as callets and finally cooled. During cooling the chocolate becomes hard and shiny so that it comes out of the moulds perfectly formed and ready for packing.

BASIC
EDIBLES &
EQUIPMENT

A good **stand mixer** makes life easier and saves valuable time.

Reliable, precise **digital scales** are better for measuring smaller quantities and are the secret to successful baking and pâtisserie. When following a recipe, use either metric or imperial weights and measures rather than a combination of both.

Heavy **mixing bowls** will make your work easier as they stay in one place and in a stable position when mixing.

High-quality, microwave-safe **plastic bowls** are a must for tempering chocolate in the microwave; other materials such as ceramic will get too hot.

It's helpful to have two different **sieves**: a fine sieve for glazes and a slightly larger one for sifting flours and

sugars to ensure your bakes have a light texture.

For best results, use a **heavy-based saucepan** as they tend to distribute heat more evenly.

Every kitchen should have a good selection of **wooden spoons and spatulas**. Silicone spatulas which are flexible enough to allow you to scrape easily around the whole bowl are great for helping to mix more evenly.

Palette knives have multiple uses, including spreading chocolate, picking up cake layers and decorative pieces, and even testing whether chocolate has been correctly tempered. Cranked palette knives are usually best they make it more comfortable and easy to spread mixtures such as sponges and mousses.

A small, **sharp knife** or craft knife has a multitude of uses so keep one to hand.

High-quality, heavy-duty **cake tins** will last you a long time without warping and will help distribute heat more evenly for the best results.

Perfect for assembling layered desserts and other dishes, **pâtisserie rings and frames** are available in a

variety of shapes and sizes. Make sure they are high-quality and don't bend.

In the catering industry we use **silicone-coated paper** for lining tins and trays when baking instead of traditional greaseproof paper. Unlike greaseproof paper, silicone paper doesn't need to be greased to make it non-stick and it gives better results. I like to use silicone baking mats which can be washed and reused over and over again.

I always say to my students that if you're having trouble baking then it's likely to be down to your oven. Always use an **oven thermometer** to get an accurate reading of the temperature inside the oven and adjust accordingly; this can make a big difference when baking.

I prefer **bristled pastry brushes** to silicone ones because they are more delicate to work with. It's worth spending a little more money on a high-quality brush that won't shed its bristles.

There is a wide variety of **silicone moulds** available, from traditional shapes to more specialist designs; you can adapt the recipes in this book to fit the moulds of your choice. The glossy surface and flexible silicone makes it easy to release food in one piece for flawless results. Choose high-quality moulds which are safe to use at a wide range of temperatures in the oven, microwave, refrigerator and freezer.

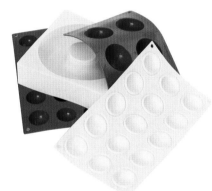

Opt for professional-standard polycarbonate **chocolate moulds** as they last forever if you look after them; just don't use anything abrasive to clean them as it will scratch the surface.

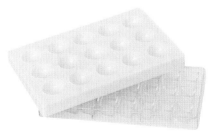

You can create a whole host of chocolate decorations using a cold **marble or granite slab**. They are inexpensive and readily available – look out for chopping boards or placemats made from marble or granite in kitchen shops and supermarkets.

Chocolate **freeze spray** or cooling spray is important for attaching petals to chocolate flowers and showpiece work. The food-grade spray rapidly cools chocolate and sugar work so you save precious time between stages.

A **chocolate scraper** is invaluable for making many different decorations and levelling moulded chocolates. Make sure that the blade is nice and flexible.

A **digital thermometer** is a must for ensuring you are working to the correct temperatures, especially for tempering chocolate and making glazes.

Use a **heat gun** to heat chocolate during and after tempering in a controlled, gradual way. If you don't have one, a hairdryer makes a good alternative.

A high-quality set of **round metal cutters** is very handy to have for cutting chocolate discs as well as many other applications.

Piping nozzles (tips) can be used in both plastic and paper piping bags. Savoy nozzles are great for piping larger amounts of mixes. Washable

plastic piping bags are a lot cleaner to use when piping chocolate: after use, place them in the refrigerator to set the chocolate so you can easily separate them and reuse both the chocolate and the bag.

Sharp **kitchen scissors** are essential for snipping the tips of piping bags, cutting silicone paper and opening packets.

A good **chocolate dipping fork** will help you dip fudge, nougat, biscuits, fruit and more into chocolate for an even covering.

All of the chocolates listed in the recipes in this book are **couverture chocolate**, which contains 32–39%

cocoa butter. This gives the chocolate a better flavour and lovely sheen and makes it easier to work with. It provides a finer finish than the more readily available confectionery chocolate, which contains vegetable fats. Confectionery chocolate isn't great quality and doesn't have a distinctive flavour so I would avoid using it for recipes.

It's important to use **fat-soluble dust food colours** when colouring melted chocolate. I use Squires Kitchen colours as they always work;

just make sure you check with the retailer that your chosen brand is suitable for chocolate.

Where the weight of eggs is important for the success of a recipe, I have given the amount in grams and ounces. The approximate number of eggs needed is also given as a guide, however I would recommend weighing the eggs so you can measure them accurately. I've used **medium and large eggs**, which in the UK are 53–

63g (2–2¼oz) and 63–73g (2¼–2½oz) respectively. Approximately two thirds of that weight is egg white and one third is yolk.

In professional kitchens we use four different types of gelatine – bronze, silver, gold and platinum – which have different bloom (setting) strengths. For recipes which require leaf gelatine, I've used Squires Kitchen **gelatine** sheets, which measure 12cm x 7cm and are bronze bloom strength. It's worth checking the strength of the gelatine you're using to ensure optimal setting of your recipes.

HISTORICAL CHOCOLATE EQUIPMENT

Antiques from the extensive Dutton Collection, selected items of which are on display in the museum at the Squires Kitchen shop in Farnham, Surrey

20th-century copper bain-marie for chocolate work

18th-century chocolatière

Late 17th-century wooden molinet for whipping hot chocolate

MASTERING
TEMPERING

The following recipes cover numerous chocolate techniques, however there's one key skill that it's important to know before you try them. Start with mastering tempering: if you conquer this then you can conquer anything. A lot of my students think tempering is difficult when they start working with chocolate but if you break it down into steps and practise, you'll succeed.

Tempering ensures the correct formation of cocoa butter crystals so that when the chocolate sets it has a good snap and shine. There are many different ways to temper chocolate but I prefer the following three methods as they all require very little specialist equipment.

It's important to use a high-quality chocolate, known as couverture, which contains 32–39% cocoa butter. This gives the chocolate a better flavour and lovely sheen, makes it easier to work with and provides a finer finish than chocolate with a lower percentage of cocoa butter. All of the chocolates listed in the recipes in this book are couverture. You can buy high-quality couverture chocolate from Squires Kitchen (see suppliers on page 192) and other reputable chocolate suppliers.

TEMPERING IN A MICROWAVE

YOU WILL NEED

High-quality couverture chocolate: milk, dark or white, chopped or in callets

Microwave (a domestic one is fine)

Plastic bowl suitable for use in the microwave

Plastic or metal spoon or spatula

Hairdryer or heat gun

Digital thermometer (optional: you can still temper chocolate without one)

Palette knife

TOP TIP

It may take you more than one attempt to get this right as all microwaves are different. Make a note of the timings for your microwave so you can refer to them next time. Take it one step at a time and don't be tempted to rush.

1 Place two thirds of the amount of the chocolate that you are going to temper into a bowl (A); the other third will be used later in the tempering process. You will need to use a microwaveable plastic bowl as porcelain will become too hot.

2 Place the bowl in the microwave and heat for 30 seconds on half power. Stir the chocolate then return it to the microwave for another 30 seconds. You will notice that the chocolate will start to melt slowly (B). Repeat this as many times as required until the chocolate has melted (C). Don't be tempted to rush this stage of the process as the chocolate may burn if heated for too long.

3 When the chocolate has melted completely it should be 40–45°C (105–115°F) – you can test this with a thermometer if you have one.

4 Add the remaining third of the chocolate a little at a time to the melted chocolate (D) and stir gently, taking care not to over-stir. The cold chocolate will melt into the warm chocolate and will lower the temperature slightly (E). You may not need to add all of it to reach the correct temperature.

5 If you have a thermometer, test the temperature of the chocolate to make sure that you have tempered it correctly (F). If the chocolate is at the following temperature then it is ready to use:

dark chocolate 31–32°C (88–90°F);
milk chocolate 29–30°C (84–86°F);
white chocolate 27–28°C (80–82°F).

6 You can also check that the chocolate is correctly tempered by dipping the end of a palette knife in the chocolate and setting it aside. If it starts to set in approximately five minutes then the chocolate is tempered and ready to use (G). If it does not set then it is still too hot.

7 If the cool chocolate does not melt, use a hairdryer or heat gun to melt it slowly, stirring at the same time (H). Take care not to overheat the chocolate: just before all the chocolate has melted, turn off the heat and let it finish melting by itself (this will prevent it from overheating).

8 If the chocolate is too hot, gently stir in more cool chocolate until it reaches the required temperature.

9 When you are working with the tempered chocolate, it may begin to cool and thicken. Use the hairdryer or heat gun to heat the chocolate just a little then check the temperature.

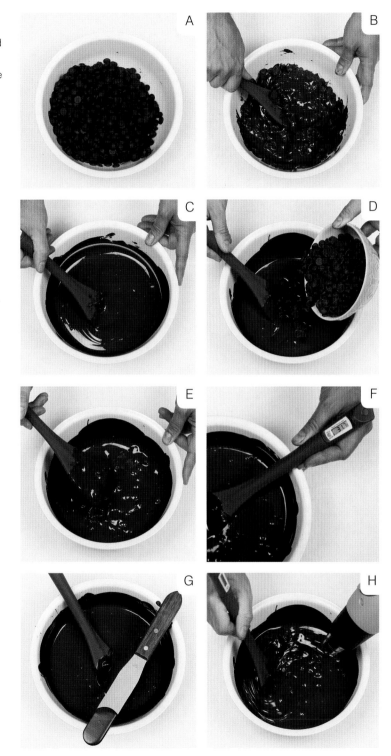

TEMPERING IN A BAIN-MARIE

YOU WILL NEED

High-quality couverture chocolate: milk, dark or white, chopped or in callets

Stove top

Saucepan

Glass bowl (that does not touch the bottom of the saucepan)

Plastic or metal spoon or spatula

Hairdryer or heat gun

Digital thermometer (optional: you can still temper chocolate without one)

Palette knife

1   Pour a small amount of water into the saucepan and bring it to a very gentle simmer.

2   Place two thirds of the amount of chocolate that you are using in the glass bowl and place this on top of the saucepan (A). Stir gently with the spatula as it melts (B).

3   When the chocolate has melted, test it with a digital thermometer if you have one: it should be approximately 40–45°C (105–115°F). Remove from the heat, wipe the underside of the glass bowl and transfer the chocolate to a plastic bowl (C).

4   Add the remaining third of the chocolate a little at a time to the melted chocolate (D) and stir gently, taking care not to over-stir. The cold chocolate will melt into the warm chocolate and will lower the temperature slightly. You may not need to add all of it to reach the correct temperature.

5   If you have a thermometer, test the temperature of the chocolate to make sure that you have tempered it correctly. If the chocolate is at the following temperature then it is ready to use:

   dark chocolate 31–32°C (88–90°F);
   milk chocolate 29–30°C (84–86°F);
   white chocolate 27–28°C (80–82°F).

6   You can also check that the chocolate is correctly tempered by dipping the end of a palette knife in the chocolate and setting it aside. If it starts to set in approximately five minutes then the chocolate is tempered and ready to use (E). If it does not set then it is still too hot.

7   If the cool chocolate does not melt, use a hairdryer or heat gun to melt it slowly, stirring at the same time. Take care not to overheat the chocolate: just before all the chocolate has melted, turn off the heat and let it finish melting by itself (this will prevent it from overheating).

8   If the chocolate is too hot, gently stir in more cool chocolate until it reaches the required temperature.

9   When you are working with the tempered chocolate, it may begin to cool and thicken. Use the hairdryer or heat gun again to heat the chocolate just a little. Check the temperature as before.

TEMPERING WITH POWDERED COCOA BUTTER

YOU WILL NEED

High-quality couverture chocolate: milk, dark or white, chopped or in callets

Powdered cocoa butter (SK): use 1% of the weight of the chocolate, e.g. 10g (½oz) for 1kg (2lb 3¼oz) of chocolate

Microwave (a domestic one is fine)

Plastic bowl suitable for use in the microwave

Plastic or metal spoon or spatula

Digital thermometer (optional: you can still temper chocolate without one

Palette knife

TOP TIP

When tempering with powdered cocoa butter you will have a longer working time before the chocolate hardens.

Pure cocoa butter in a dry powder form can also be used for frying and as a setting agent in mousses.

1 Place all of the chocolate in a plastic bowl and heat in the microwave on half power for 30 seconds. Stir the chocolate (A) then return it to the microwave for another 30 seconds. Repeat this as many times as required until the chocolate has melted (B). If you have a thermometer, check that the temperature of the chocolate is 40–45°C (105–115°F).

2 Remove the chocolate from the microwave and allow it to cool slightly. For dark chocolate, cool to 34–35°C (93–95°F); for milk, white or coloured chocolate cool to 33–34°C (91–93°F).

3 Add the powdered cocoa butter to the chocolate (C) and mix well.

4 Allow the chocolate to cool further until it is at the correct working temperature, as follows:
    dark chocolate 31–32°C (88–90°F);
    milk chocolate 29–30°C (84–86°F);
    white chocolate 27–28°C (80–82°F).
If the chocolate is at the correct temperature then it is ready to use (D).

5 You can also check that the chocolate is correctly tempered by dipping the end of a palette knife in the chocolate and setting it aside. If it starts to set in approximately five minutes then the chocolate is tempered and ready to use (E). If the chocolate does not set then it is still too hot and should be left a little longer to cool.

BITE-SIZE

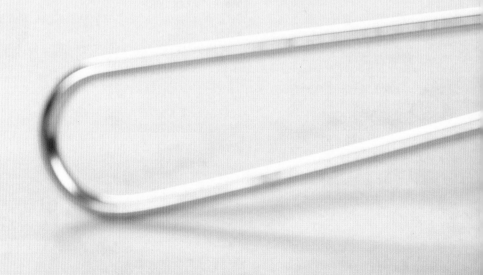

PISTACHIO & CHOCOLATE
ICE CREAMS

This recipe combines two of my favourite ingredients. The white chocolate covering contains extra cocoa butter, which allows it to set quickly over the ice cream and prevents it from breaking in extremely cold temperatures. Together with the pistachios, this gives the ice cream a beautifully crunchy texture.

INGREDIENTS

Milk Chocolate Ice Cream

50g (1¾oz) caster sugar

35g (1¼oz) egg yolks (approximately 2 large eggs)

135g (4¾oz) milk chocolate, chopped or in callets

195ml (6¾fl oz) semi-skimmed milk

100ml (3½fl oz) whipping cream

Crystallised Pistachios

125g (4½oz) pistachio nuts, finely chopped

90g (3oz) caster sugar

Pistachio Paste

100g (3½oz) pistachio nuts

1tbsp nut oil

White Chocolate Covering

600g (1lb 5¼oz) white chocolate, chopped or in callets

60g (2oz) cocoa butter

1–2tsp Fern green dust food colour (SK)

EQUIPMENT

Basic equipment (see page 18)

Ice cream maker

15-cavity globe silicone mould (Silikomart)

15 wooden lollipop sticks

MAKES 15 INDIVIDUAL ICE CREAMS

MILK CHOCOLATE ICE CREAM PREPARATION

1 Whisk the sugar and egg yolks together in a mixing bowl. Place the chocolate in a separate mixing bowl.

2 Place the milk and cream in a saucepan and bring to the boil (A).

3 Pour the hot liquid onto the egg mixture, stirring with a whisk (B). Return the mixture to the saucepan (C) and cook over a low heat for another two to three minutes, stirring continuously to avoid burning, until the mixture has thickened and coats the back of a spoon.

4 Remove the mixture from the heat and pour it over the chocolate (D), stirring with a whisk (E) until fully incorporated. Decant into a jug and leave to cool at room temperature, then cover the jug with cling film and leave to fully cool in the refrigerator overnight.

CRYSTALLISED PISTACHIOS

5 Roast the chopped nuts in an oven preheated to 160°C (325°F/gas mark 3) for approximately five minutes to bring out the flavour and to add extra crunch.

6 Heat the sugar and 25ml (>¾fl oz) of water in a small saucepan to 119°C (246°F). You may need to tilt the saucepan to get an accurate reading on the thermometer. Once at the right temperature, add the pistachios to the saucepan (F) and stir over the heat until the mixture has a sandy, dry texture (G). Remove from the heat and turn out the nuts onto a tray lined with silicone paper or a heatproof mat. Leave to cool.

TOP TIP

If some of the sugar doesn't stick to the nuts, remove it using a sieve so it doesn't make the ice cream too sweet when mixed in.

PISTACHIO PASTE

7 Blend the nuts and oil to a paste in a small food processor; this can take up to five minutes. Scrape down the sides of the processor from time to time if necessary.

MILK CHOCOLATE ICE CREAM FREEZING

8 Place the chilled ice cream mixture into an ice cream maker (H). Churn until smooth, very cold and thickened (I). Add half of the pistachio nuts

followed by the pistachio paste (J), then churn for a couple of cycles until evenly distributed.

TOP TIP

If your ice cream maker struggles to churn after the nuts are added, mix them in by hand instead.

9   Transfer the mixture to a large piping bag. Snip off the end and pipe the ice cream into the globe moulds (K). Place in the freezer for an hour or until set hard.

WHITE CHOCOLATE COVERING

10   Remove the ice creams from the mould and insert a wooden lollipop stick into the side of each one. If you find this difficult, release one side of the mould to insert the stick before fully removing the ice cream, or simply insert the sticks straight down into the top of the moulded ice cream.

11   Place the ice creams on a tray lined with silicone paper and return them to the freezer for 30 minutes.

12   Warm the white chocolate and cocoa butter together in a microwave or bain-marie until just melted but not too hot. Pour it into a small bowl.

13   Remove the ice creams from the freezer and dip into the warm chocolate (L), pulling them straight back out (M). Sprinkle with nuts on both sides (N) then place back onto the tray and return to the freezer for 10 minutes.

14   If necessary, warm the white chocolate covering as before to achieve a dipping consistency. Colour a quarter of the remaining white chocolate covering with the green dust food colour. Place it in a large piping bag, snip off the end and pipe it randomly over the surface of the uncoloured white chocolate covering (O).

15   Remove the ice creams from the freezer and dip them into the chocolate (P), swirling them around to create a green marbled effect (Q). Place the ice creams back onto the tray and return to the freezer for at least 10 minutes before serving.

16   If you're not planning to eat the ice creams immediately, store them in an airtight container with a layer of silicone paper in between each one for up to one month.

PISTACHIO AND CHOCOLATE ICE CREAMS

HOT CHOCOLATE & WHISKY
TRUFFLES

These are truffles with a difference. The centre is warm, melting and silky-smooth – a bit like a chocolate fondant on a stick. You could even get guests to dip and fry their own in a hot oil fondue pot for a special dinner party dessert.

INGREDIENTS

Truffles

100ml (3½fl oz) whipping cream

½tsp vanilla paste

50ml (1¾fl oz) whisky

250g (8¾oz) dark chocolate, chopped or in callets

50g (1¾oz) butter, cubed

Pinch of salt

Batter

50g (1¾oz) cocoa powder

250g (8¾oz) plain flour

2g (⅛oz) salt

50g (1¾oz) caster sugar

300ml (10½fl oz) sparkling wine

120g (4¼oz) eggs (approximately 2 large eggs)

50g (1¾oz) unsalted butter, melted

1l (1¾pt) vegetable oil, for frying

EQUIPMENT

Basic equipment (see page 18)

25 x 30cm (12") wooden barbecue skewers

TRUFFLES

1   Heat the cream in a saucepan with the vanilla paste and whisky until just about to boil. Remove from the heat and allow to cool slightly for a minute.

2   Place the chocolate in a mixing bowl and pour the cream over the top (A). Whisk out from the centre (B) to achieve a nice emulsion (C). You may have to scrape around the sides of the bowl occasionally to incorporate all of the cream with the chocolate. If the chocolate has not fully melted, heat it in a microwave in short bursts or over a bain-marie.

3   Whisk the butter and salt through the mixture (D) until fully incorporated.

4   Place the ganache in the base of an airtight container and lay cling film directly over the surface of the ganache. Allow it to cool to room temperature then place the lid on top and leave it to set in the refrigerator for at least one hour.

5   Once set, use a teaspoon or melon baller to scoop out truffle-sized portions of ganache (E), about 3cm (1⅛") in diameter or 20g (¾oz) each. If necessary, roll them between your hands to create spherical truffles; it is best to wear food-safe plastic gloves for this stage (F). (The truffles can be made larger; they would just need to be fried for longer.) Place on a tray and leave to set in the refrigerator for 30 minutes.

6   When the truffles are firm, insert the blunt end of a wooden skewer into each one; if you use the sharp end, the truffle will slide down the stick when it is fried. Place them in the freezer for at least two hours until fully frozen. At this point, you can freeze the truffles for up to a month in an airtight container with silicone paper between them.

BATTER

7   Place the cocoa powder, flour, salt and caster sugar together in a large bowl (G). Make a well in the centre of the dry mixture and gradually add the sparkling wine (H), whisking continuously (I) until fully combined.

8   Add the eggs (J) and whisk until fully combined. Whisk in the melted butter (K) until fully combined (L). If you find the mixture too stiff, beat it in a stand mixer fitted with a paddle attachment instead. Leave to set in the refrigerator for an hour. At this point, you can freeze the batter for up to a month in an airtight container.

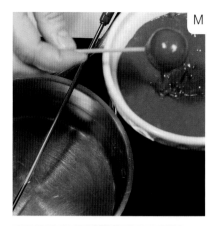

FRYING

9 On the day of serving, pour the vegetable oil into a large saucepan until it reaches approximately 5cm (2") below the rim of the pan.

10 Heat the oil to approximately 170°C (340°F), using a thermometer to check the temperature. Try to keep the oil at this temperature throughout the cooking.

11 Remove the batter from the refrigerator and stir to help it become a little looser.

12 Remove the truffles from the freezer. Working in pairs, hold the truffles by their skewers, dip them into the batter until completely covered (M) then remove any drips on the side of the bowl.

13 Place the truffles in the hot oil to cook: start by swirling each one around to form a neat sphere. Fry for approximately three to four minutes (N). Once you are confident, you could have up to three pairs at a time in the oil as long as you can keep track of when each pair started cooking.

TOP TIP

If a truffle starts leaking, check that the oil is not too hot. It could also mean that the truffle was not completely coated in batter or that you are leaving the truffles in the oil for too long.

14 Remove the truffle from the oil (O) and place on a tray lined with kitchen paper. Leave to cool slightly then dust with cocoa powder just before serving.

TOP TIP

If you find plain cocoa powder too bitter, try mixing with an equal amount of icing sugar before dusting the truffles.

CHOCOLATE, MAPLE & BACON
MACAROONS

I discovered the magical combination of smooth chocolate, sweet maple syrup and salty, crispy bacon when I was on holiday in America. I couldn't wait to try it in one of my own recipes: this is the result.

INGREDIENTS

Chocolate Macaroons

150g (5¼oz) icing sugar

15g (½oz) cocoa powder

135g (4¾oz) ground almonds

110g (4oz) egg whites (approximately
3 large eggs)

165g (5½oz) caster sugar

Bacon Sprinkle

120g (4¼oz) streaky bacon
(approximately 6 rashers)

Maple Buttercream

80g (2¾oz) egg whites (approximately
2 large eggs)

50g (1¾oz) caster sugar

3tbsp maple syrup

170g (5¾oz) unsalted butter, softened

Decoration

50g (1¾oz) white chocolate,
tempered

EQUIPMENT

Basic equipment (see page 18)

Macaroon baking mat with 3cm (1⅛")
guidelines (optional)

Round piping nozzles: 5mm and 1cm
(¼" and ⅜")

MAKES 40–50 MACAROONS

CHOCOLATE MACAROONS

1   Mix the icing sugar, cocoa powder and ground almonds together then transfer to a food processor and briefly blitz into a very fine powder.

2   Sift the powder through a fine sieve (A). Stir in 55g (2oz) of egg whites to make a paste (B–D).

3   Place the remaining 55g (2oz) of egg whites into the bowl of a stand mixer. Using the whisk attachment, whisk the whites until they reach soft peaks, then whisk in 15g (½oz) of caster sugar (E).

TOP TIP

If the amount of egg whites is too small for your stand mixer at first, use a hand beater in the stand mixer bowl to increase the volume of the whites before switching to the stand mixer.

4   Meanwhile, heat the remaining 150g (5¼oz) of caster sugar with 40ml (1½fl oz) of water in a saucepan to 118°C (244°F) (F).

5   Continuing to whisk the egg whites in the stand mixer at a medium speed, gradually add the boiled sugar in a thin stream (G) until the mixture becomes thick, glossy and cool to the touch – this should take approximately 10 minutes.

6   Fold a third of the cooled egg whites into the nut paste to loosen the paste (H). Then fold in the remaining egg whites (I) until the mixture is shiny and has the consistency of a thick paste (J) – see the Top Tip below.

TOP TIP

This stage of the mixture is crucial for successful macaroons. Spoon a little of the mixture onto a flat surface: it should sink slowly of its own accord without any peaks. If the mixture spreads quickly like a liquid, it has been over-mixed.

7   Line a baking tray with silicone paper or a macaroon baking mat. Secure the lining by piping a dot of macaroon mixture onto the corners of the tray beneath it, then press the lining down to stop it from sliding around as you pipe. Fit a piping bag with a 5mm (¼") round nozzle and fill the piping bag with the mixture. Pipe 2cm (¾") circles onto the tray, leaving at least a 2cm (¾") gap between each one (K). Tap the tray on the work surface to release any air bubbles: I do this by dropping the tray

from a short distance above the surface. The macaroons should spread to 3cm (1¹/₈").

8   Leave to crust over for 30–40 minutes (L), or until the tops are no longer sticky; this may be quicker or slower depending on the humidity in the kitchen. Meanwhile, preheat the oven to 140°C (275°F/gas mark 1).

9   Bake in the oven for 15–20 minutes, or until firm on top. Remove from the oven and allow to cool completely before taking the macaroons off the tray.

TOP TIP

At this point the unfilled macaroons can be stored between layers of greaseproof paper in an airtight container in the refrigerator for up to four days or in the freezer for up to two months.

BACON SPRINKLE

10   Place the bacon rashers on a lined baking tray. Bake in a preheated oven at 110°C (225°F/gas mark ¼) for 45–60 minutes or until dried and crisp, turning halfway through the cooking time.

11   Remove from the oven, soak up any grease with kitchen paper if the bacon is oily and leave it to cool.

12   Place the bacon in a food blender or spice grinder and blend to a powder.

MAPLE BUTTERCREAM

13   Combine the egg whites, sugar and 1tbsp of maple syrup in the heatproof bowl of a stand mixer. Place it over a saucepan of water to form a bain-marie, making sure the bowl doesn't touch the water.

14   Heat to approximately 60°C (140°F) or until warm to the touch, making sure to stir the mixture from time to time so the eggs don't scramble (M).

15   Remove the bowl from the bain-marie, place it on the stand mixer and beat with the whisk attachment until light, fluffy and cooled to room temperature – approximately 10 minutes at a medium speed (N, O).

16   Gradually add the butter a little at a time (P) until it is all incorporated. If the mixture starts to curdle, keep whisking it on a slow speed until it reaches the correct consistency.

17   Mix two thirds of the bacon sprinkle into the buttercream along with 2tbsp of maple syrup (Q). Transfer the buttercream to a piping bag fitted with a 1cm (³/₈") nozzle.

ASSEMBLY

18   Pipe buttercream onto half of the macaroons then place the remaining halves on top (R).

19   Place the white chocolate into a small paper piping bag. Snip off the very end and pipe fine lines over one side of the macaroons (S). Before the chocolate sets, sprinkle the rest of the bacon over it (T) then leave to set.

20   Once they are filled, store the macaroons between layers of greaseproof paper in an airtight container in the refrigerator for up to four days.

CHOCOLATE DOUGHNUTS

WITH A MALTED MILK CENTRE

These delicious doughnuts are best served warm so the comforting
malted milk filling oozes out when you take a bite.

INGREDIENTS

Chocolate Doughnuts

140ml (5fl oz) milk

1tsp dried active yeast

115g (4oz) unsalted butter, softened and cubed

25g (¾oz) caster sugar

155g (5½oz) plain flour, plus a little extra for dusting

155g (5½oz) strong white bread flour

40g (1½oz) cocoa powder

½tsp salt

90g (3oz) whole eggs, beaten, at room temperature (approximately 2 medium eggs)

1l (1¾pt) vegetable oil, for frying

150g (5¼oz) caster sugar

½tsp cinnamon

½tsp Gold Sparkles dust food colour (SK)

Malted Milk Filling

80g (2¾oz) egg yolks (approximately 4 large eggs)

50g (1¾oz) caster sugar

20g (¾oz) cornflour

50g (1¾oz) malt extract

30g (1oz) malted drink powder

300ml (10½fl oz) semi-skimmed milk

½tsp vanilla bean paste

EQUIPMENT

Basic equipment (see page 18)

5cm (2") circular cutter

5mm (¼") round, plain piping nozzle

MAKES 20–25 DOUGHNUTS

CHOCOLATE DOUGHNUTS

1   Warm the milk slightly, then add the yeast and leave it to dissolve.

2   Cream the butter and caster sugar together in the bowl of a stand mixer. Add the flours, cocoa powder and salt (A) and mix to a crumb. If the mixture is too thick, start adding the warm milk at this stage.

3   Add the rest of the warm milk and eggs (B) and mix again briefly, scraping down the beater and sides of the bowl to ensure it is fully incorporated (C, D).

4   Fit the mixer with a dough hook and knead the mixture at a medium speed for 10–12 minutes until all the ingredients are well combined and a dough has formed.

5   Place the dough in a floured bowl, cover with cling film and leave in a warm place, e.g. an airing cupboard, to double in size. This should take one to two hours.

TOP TIP

If you don't have a proving drawer or another suitable place like an airing cupboard, heat a bowl of water in the microwave for five minutes, then remove the water and place the dough inside to prove with the door closed and power turned off. If you use this method, you just need to make sure that the bowl or tray holding the dough will fit in the microwave.

6   Roll out the dough to approximately 1.5cm (½") thick on a lightly floured surface (E). Cut out 5cm (2") discs using a circular cutter; they should weigh 25–30g (¾–1oz) each (F). Roll each disc between your palms or on a work surface to make them all into balls (G). Place them on an oiled baking tray and cover with cling film oiled using a spray bottle, pastry brush or some kitchen paper. Leave in a warm place to double in size again; this can take up to one hour.

TOP TIP

You can freeze the uncooked, unproved dough balls for up to a month. When ready to use, simply remove the dough and let it double in size; this stage of proving will just take a little longer.

CHOCOLATE DOUGHNUTS WITH A MALTED MILK CENTRE

7 Pour the vegetable oil into a large saucepan until it reaches approximately 5cm (2") below the rim of the pan. Heat the oil to 180°C (356°F), using a thermometer to check the temperature. Try to keep the oil at this temperature throughout cooking.

TOP TIP

When the oil reaches 180°C (356°F), turn down the heat slightly to help the oil maintain the correct temperature.

8 Place four doughnuts, one at a time rather than all at once, into the hot oil (H, see page 49). Fry for eight to 10 minutes until they are a darker chocolate colour but not black, moving them around slowly using a heat-proof utensil such as a fork to make sure they are evenly cooked (I, see page 49).

9 Meanwhile, mix the caster sugar, cinnamon and gold dust food colour together in a bowl.

10 Remove the doughnuts from the oil with a slotted spoon and place them on some kitchen paper on a tray for a few minutes to soak up the oil. Place them in the bowl of cinnamon sugar, rotating them until they are completely coated (J–L). Leave to cool on a tray at room temperature before filling.

MALTED MILK FILLING

11 Lightly whisk the egg yolks, sugar, cornflour, malt extract and malted drink powder together in a small bowl.

12 Place the milk and vanilla in a saucepan and bring to the boil. Remove from the heat and pour onto the egg mixture, whisking continuously to prevent the eggs from scrambling.

13 Return the mixture to the saucepan and cook it on a low heat until it thickens, stirring continuously. Continue to gently simmer and stir for two to three minutes. Remove from the heat and transfer to a shallow container or tray to help it cool quickly.

14 Leave to cool at room temperature for 10 minutes then place a small piece of cling film directly on top of the filling and leave it to cool in the fridge for 45 minutes.

15 When the doughnuts and malted milk filling are both cool, transfer the filling into a large piping bag fitted with a 5mm (¼") round nozzle. Make a hole in the centre of the doughnut using the tip of a long, thin knife: wiggle it around inside the doughnut to create some more space inside. Insert the piping nozzle into the hole and squeeze the filling inside until it reaches the outer edge.

16 These doughnuts can be stored in an airtight container for a day or two but they are best served on the same day when they are as fresh as possible.

PASSION FRUIT
CHOCOLATES

You could say these are the perfect chocolates for summer, but I think that the combination of smooth, dark chocolate and zingy passion fruit is a winner at any time of year. If you can't source fresh passion fruits, you could also make the purée by reducing passion fruit juice by 50%.

INGREDIENTS

Passion Fruit Purée

200g (7oz) passion fruit pulp
(approximately 9 fruits)

25g (>¾oz) caster sugar

1tsp lemon juice

Chocolate Shells

Professional Cocol cocoa butter
colourings: orange, white and
yellow (SK)

1kg (2lb 3¼oz) dark chocolate

Passion Fruit Ganache

50ml (1¾fl oz) whipping cream

100g (3½oz) passion fruit purée
(see recipe above)

25g (>¾oz) liquid glucose

90g (3oz) milk chocolate

70g (2½oz) dark chocolate

20g (¾oz) unsalted butter, cut into
small pieces

EQUIPMENT

Basic equipment (see page 18)

2 x 24-cavity polycarbonate chocolate
moulds

MAKES 48 CHOCOLATES

PASSION FRUIT PURÉE

1 Extract the pulp (pips and all) from the fruits into a small bowl.

2 Bring the sugar and 25ml (>¾fl oz) of water to the boil in a small saucepan. Add the fruit pulp and simmer for five minutes, stirring occasionally.

3 Remove from the heat and pass the purée through a fine sieve into a bowl. Use the back of a soup ladle to extract as much of the juice and pulp as possible. Scrape the underside of the sieve to capture all of the purée.

4 Add the lemon juice. Cover the bowl with cling film and set aside to cool until required.

SHELLS

5 Make sure the two moulds are clean and free from grease and water. Line your worktop with greaseproof paper to help protect it from the cocoa butter splatters.

> ### TOP TIP
>
> Use a lint-free cloth such as a glass cloth to clean the chocolate moulds; avoid using cotton wool as it leaves fibres behind.

6 Heat the three colours of cocoa butter so they're slightly warm, but not hot. If using Cocol cocoa butter colours, remove the lids and microwave separately on full power until the contents have melted fully. Remove from the microwave, replace the lids and shake at regular intervals to ensure even temperature distribution. Alternatively, melt the Cocol by placing the bottles in warm water.

7 Mix a little of the white cocoa butter colouring into the orange and yellow as this makes the colours more vibrant and helps make them stand out against the dark chocolate. Use a pastry brush or a new and unused toothbrush to splatter each mould with the two colours of cocoa butter, one after the other (A, B).

8 Leave the two colours to dry and go matt for approximately three to five minutes. Use a chocolate scraper to scrape the cocoa butter off the top of the mould (C), then use a soft cloth to clean off any remaining residue.

A

B

C

9 Temper 1kg (2lb 3¼oz) of dark chocolate. Transfer to a large piping bag, snip off the end and pipe the chocolate into each cavity of the two moulds as quickly as you can (D).

10 Use a scraper to scrape the excess chocolate from the top of the mould (E). Tap the moulds on the worktop to release any air bubbles from the surface of the mould.

11 Turn the moulds upside down one at a time to release the excess chocolate (F). Tap the side of the mould with a scraper, keeping the mould level at all times (G). Once the chocolate has stopped dripping, scrape the mould again, this time whilst it is upside down, so the excess chocolate falls out of the mould (H).

12 Turn the moulds upright and clean with scraper again (I, J). Place the moulds upside down on a piece of silicone paper until the chocolate is touch-dry, then place in the fridge to fully set for no more than 30 minutes. Remove from the fridge.

PASSION FRUIT GANACHE

13 To make the ganache, bring the cream, purée and glucose to the boil in a saucepan, stirring with a whisk to prevent the cream from burning (K). Remove it from the heat and leave to reach 38°C (100°F).

14 Meanwhile, gently heat the dark and milk chocolate in a bain-marie or microwave until it reaches 32°C (90°F).

15 Pour the cream mixture into the chocolate (L) and use a whisk to gradually combine the two mixtures (M, N). Stir the butter into the ganache (O) until melted and fully combined (P).

ASSEMBLY

16 Transfer the ganache to a large piping bag, snip off the end and pipe into the chocolate shells, filling them to 2–3mm (¹/₁₆–¹/₈") from the top (Q). Leave the chocolates to set overnight at room temperature.

17 Temper approximately 200g (7oz) of the leftover dark chocolate and transfer it to a large piping bag.

18 Use a heat gun to heat the exposed side of the chocolates, melting the chocolate around the edges slightly (R).

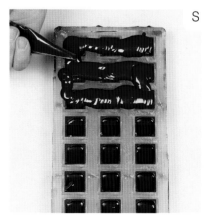

19 Pipe some of the tempered dark chocolate over the first three rows of chocolates (S), then scrape the dark chocolate downwards to fill all of the

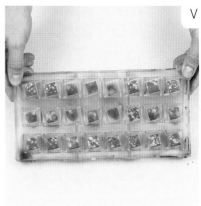

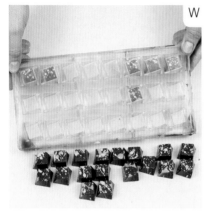

chocolates (T, U). Clean off the sides and tap the moulds on the worktop to release any air bubbles. Repeat this process if the tops are not completely clean.

20   Set aside at room temperature until the freshly piped chocolate is touch-dry, then place in the refrigerator for 20 minutes to set.

21   Remove the chocolates by turning over the moulds and tapping the edge furthest away from you on the work surface (V). Tap different edges until the mould is empty (W).

22   Store in an airtight container in the refrigerator for up to a week. They can also be frozen in an airtight container for up to three months: allow to fully defrost in the refrigerator before opening the container. In both cases, make sure they reach room temperature before eating.

Mark outside L'Ecole de Boulangerie et de Pâtisserie de Paris where he practised for a week before competing in the World Chocolate Masters in 2009.

CHOCOLATE
NOUGAT
BARS

I love the texture of this nougat: not too hard, not too chewy, it contrasts beautifully with the crunch of the nuts and cocoa nibs. The all-important addition of chocolate, both inside and outside, complements the fruit and nuts to create a flavour sensation.

INGREDIENTS

Chocolate Nougat

50g (1¾oz) blanched almonds

50g (1¾oz) skinned hazelnuts

50g (1¾oz) pistachio nuts

10g (¼oz) cocoa nibs

60g (2oz) egg whites (approximately 2 medium eggs)

½tsp vanilla paste

350g (12¼oz) caster sugar

½tsp cream of tartar

100g (3½oz) liquid glucose

100g (3½oz) honey

150g (5¼oz) dark chocolate, chopped or in callets

100g (3½oz) mixed dried fruits, e.g. raisins, cranberries, papaya, pineapple

Chocolate Covering

2kg (4lb 6½oz) dark chocolate, tempered

2tsp Copper dust food colour (SK)

EQUIPMENT

Basic equipment (see page 18)

Square, loose-bottomed sandwich tin, 4cm (1½") deep: 20.5cm (8")

CHOCOLATE NOUGAT

1 Grease and line a 20.5cm (8") square sandwich tin with silicone paper. Preheat the oven to 80°C (175°F, gas mark low).

2 Place the almonds, hazelnuts, pistachios and cocoa nibs on a baking tray and bake in the oven for 15–20 minutes until lightly roasted.

3 Meanwhile, place the egg whites and vanilla paste in the bowl of a stand mixer fitted with the whisk attachment. In a small bowl, stir 20g (¾oz) of the caster sugar together with the cream of tartar. Add the sugar mixture to the egg whites and whisk at a medium speed until they reach stiff-peak consistency.

4 Place the rest of the sugar with the glucose, honey and 75ml (2½fl oz) of water in a large saucepan and bring to the boil. Keep the mixture at a rolling boil until it reaches 149°C (300°F), stirring occasionally (A).

5 Once it has reached temperature, gradually pour the liquid into the egg white mixture (B). Whisk for three minutes at a medium speed (C).

6 Add the dark chocolate (D) and continue whisking until it has melted (E) and is fully incorporated.

7 Transfer the mixture to the prepared tin (F). Use a spatula or an oiled piece of silicone paper to ensure the mixture is level all the way into the corners of the tin (G).

8 Stir the roasted nuts and nibs together with the mixed dried fruits. Push them gently on top of the mixture in the tin (H) until you have achieved an even, single layer (I). Set aside to cool and set for two hours.

CHOCOLATE COVERING

9 Remove the set nougat from the tin, turn it over so the base is facing upwards and peel off the silicone paper (J). Spread a fine layer (approximately 2mm/¹⁄₁₆") of tempered dark chocolate on the bottom with a palette knife (K). Leave to set for 10 minutes at room temperature (L).

TOP TIP

2kg (4lb 6½oz) may seem like a lot of chocolate: you will have excess but this amount is needed for dipping. The leftover chocolate can be set and stored for another recipe; simply re-temper it when needed.

CHOCOLATE NOUGAT BARS

64

10   Cut the nougat into 20 bars measuring approximately 10cm x 2cm (4" x ¾") with a large, sharp knife, keeping the lines as straight as possible.

11   Place one bar at a time, coated side down, into the tempered chocolate (M). Use a dipping fork to pull chocolate over the top of the bar until it is completely covered (N). Slide the fork two thirds of the way under the bar and lift it out of the chocolate (O).

12   Hold the fork with the coated bar above the chocolate, moving it up and down slightly, to allow the excess chocolate to fall back into the bowl. Tap the fork gently on the side of the bowl and, finally, scrape the bottom of the coated bar along the edge of the bowl as you lift it out, to prevent it from dripping. Place the coated nougat bar onto a sheet of acetate or silicone paper (P).

13   Repeat steps 11–12 for all of the bars. Place the bars in the fridge to set for 15 minutes, then remove and brush with little copper dust food colour (Q).

14   Store the nougat in an airtight container in a cool, dry place for up to two weeks.

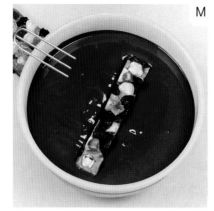

M

N

O

P

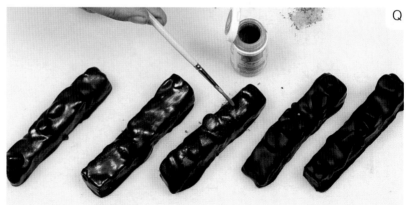

Q

MILK CHOCOLATE &
EARL GREY TEA
FUDGE

Hot or cold cream infusions are a great way to create new depths of flavour in your chocolate work, for example in ganaches. In this recipe I infuse cream with Earl Grey tea as I find the floral and citrus flavours work beautifully with milk chocolate. And once you know how to make your own chocolate transfer sheets, you can use this method to personalise lots of your chocolate creations.

INGREDIENTS

Fudge

20g (¾oz) loose-leaf Earl Grey tea

250ml (8¾fl oz) whipping cream, plus
a little extra

200g (7oz) milk chocolate, chopped
or in callets

400g (14oz) caster sugar

120g (4¼oz) liquid glucose

60g (2oz) butter

Coating

Professional Cocol cocoa butter
colouring: sapphire (SK)

2kg (4lb 6½oz) dark chocolate,
tempered

EQUIPMENT

Basic equipment (see page 18)

Square, loose-bottomed sandwich tin:
20.5cm (8")

25.5cm x 25.5cm (10" x 10")
acetate sheet

2.5cm (1") cube of new washing-up
sponge

MAKES 100 CHOCOLATES

FUDGE

1 Grease and line a 20.5cm (8") square sandwich tin with silicone paper. (It's best to use a sandwich tin as deeper ones can make it harder to level the fudge.)

2 Stir the tea into 250ml (8¾fl oz) of cream and leave it in the refrigerator for at least one hour, ideally overnight.

TOP TIP

The tea leaves will absorb some of the cream, leaving you with less than you started with once it has been strained. If you don't quite have the right amount, you can make up the difference with uninfused whipping cream.

3 Strain the tea and cream through a fine sieve, pushing as much of the cream through as possible using a balloon whisk or soup ladle (A). Measure 150ml (5¼fl oz) of tea-infused cream; if it is under, add a little extra uninfused cream to make it up to the correct amount.

4 Place the milk chocolate in a large bowl (B).

5 Heat the tea-infused cream along with the sugar, glucose and butter in a large saucepan (C) to 106°C (223°F), stirring to combine (D).

6 Remove from the heat and pour the mixture over the milk chocolate (E). Stir until the chocolate has melted and is fully incorporated (F).

7 Transfer the fudge mixture to the lined tin (G) and level it with the back of a spoon (H). Allow to cool to room temperature then leave in the refrigerator for two hours or until set.

COATING

8 Heat the cocoa butter colouring so it's slightly warm, but not hot. If using Cocol cocoa butter colouring, remove the lid and microwave on full power until the contents have melted fully. Remove from the microwave, replace the lid and shake at regular intervals to ensure even temperature distribution. Alternatively, melt the Cocol by placing the bottle in warm water.

9 Brush a fine layer of the cocoa butter colouring over the acetate sheet (I, J). Leave it to set at room temperature until dry and matt, then brush on another layer.

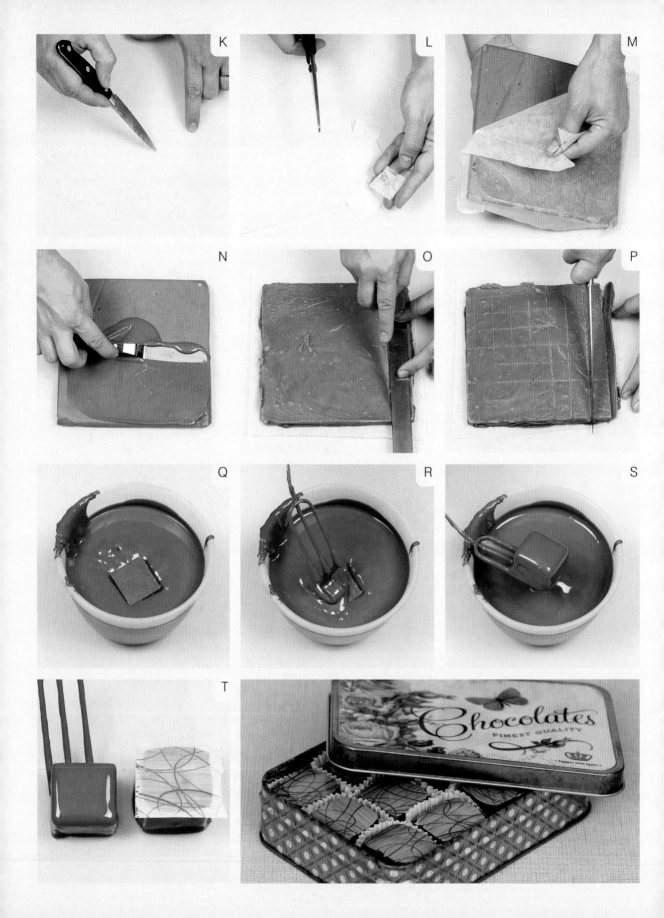

10   Leave it to set again at room temperature for five minutes. Once set, use the tip of a sharp knife to etch a pattern of swirled lines into the cocoa butter (K). Cut the acetate sheet into 2.5cm (1") squares (L).

11   Take the fudge out of the refrigerator, remove it from the tin and peel off the lining (M). Spread a thin layer of tempered dark chocolate on top of the fudge (N) and leave it to set at room temperature for 10 minutes.

12   Turn the fudge over and cut it into 2cm (¾") squares with a warm, sharp knife (O, P).

TOP TIP

To cut the fudge with smooth, clean lines, place the knife in a jug of hot, boiled water. Dry it with some kitchen paper before cutting, then replace in the water for a few seconds and dry before making the next cut.

13   Place one piece of fudge at a time, coated side down, into the tempered chocolate (Q). Use a dipping fork to pull chocolate over the top of the fudge (R) until it is completely covered. Slide the fork under the fudge and lift it out of the chocolate (S).

14   Hold the fork with the fudge above the chocolate, tapping the surface of the chocolate very lightly to remove any excess chocolate and prevent a 'foot' forming when placed on the acetate. Then tap the fork gently on the side of the bowl and, finally, scrape it on the edge of the bowl as you lift it out, to prevent it from dripping. Place the coated fudge onto a sheet of acetate or silicone paper, sliding out the fork as you do so.

15   Before the chocolate sets, place one of the prepared 2.5cm (1") acetate squares, cocoa butter side down, on top of the piece of coated fudge. Press down on the acetate with a 2.5cm (1") cube of washing-up sponge to ensure it lies flat against the whole surface.

16   Repeat steps 14–15 to cover all of the fudge (T). If the chocolate starts to thicken, heat it with a heat gun as per the tempering instructions on page 22. Place the covered fudge in the refrigerator to set for 30 minutes, then peel away the acetate squares to leave the cocoa butter design behind.

17   Store the fudge in an airtight container in a cool, dry place for up to two weeks.

INDIVIDUAL

CHOCOLATE ORANGE & PISTACHIO
OPÉRA CAKE

A traditional gateau opéra is an almond sponge cake with a coffee and chocolate icing and filling – a must-have in any pastry chef's repertoire. I've updated the recipe, replacing coffee with orange to add a zesty flavour and a colourful, contemporary glaze.

INGREDIENTS

Chocolate Glaze

10g (¼oz) leaf gelatine (6 leaves)

150g (5¼oz) liquid glucose

150g (5¼oz) caster sugar

100g (3½oz) condensed milk

150g (5¼oz) white chocolate

½tsp Orange dust food colour (SK)

Almond Sponge

100g (3½oz) blanched almonds

85g (2¾oz) pistachio nuts

220g (7¾oz) caster sugar

45g (1½oz) plain flour

35g (1¼oz) unsalted butter, melted

2 large eggs, whole

4 large eggs, separated

Pinch of salt

Dark Chocolate Ganache

200g (7oz) dark chocolate

150ml (5¼fl oz) whipping cream

1 orange, zest only

Orange Syrup

50g (1¾fl oz) caster sugar

1 orange, zest and juice

Orange Buttercream

2 large egg whites

100g (3½oz) caster sugar

170g (5¾oz) butter, softened to a spreadable consistency

2 oranges, zest and 2 tbsp juice

Chocolate Decorations

Cocktail Dots Designer Transfer Sheet for Chocolate (SK): ½ a sheet; 30cm x 10cm (12" x 4")

100g (3½oz) white chocolate, tempered

Crystallised Pistachios

125g (4½oz) pistachio nuts

90g (3oz) caster sugar

EQUIPMENT

Basic equipment (see page 18)

3 x baking trays: 38cm x 33cm (15" x 13")

GLAZE

1   Soak the gelatine in 60ml (2oz) of water for 10 minutes.

2   Place 75ml (2½oz) of water along with the liquid glucose, sugar and condensed milk in a saucepan and heat to 103°C (217°F) (A).

3   Reduce the heat, then add the soaked gelatine and any leftover water (B). Remove from the heat and use a hand blender to blend the mixture (C).

4   Add the white chocolate (D) and blend until melted (E). Add the orange dust food colour (F) and blend again until fully incorporated (G).

5   Pour the mixture through a fine sieve. Transfer to an airtight container, allow to cool to room temperature then place in the refrigerator to set overnight.

ALMOND SPONGE

6   Preheat the oven to 210°C (410°F/gas mark 6). Line three baking trays with baking parchment, securing it either with a non-stick spray or by brushing the tray with cooking oil.

7   Blend the almonds, pistachios and 185g (6½oz) of caster sugar in a food processor to a fine powder.

8   Transfer the nut mixture to the bowl of a stand mixer and add the flour, butter, two whole eggs and four egg yolks. Using the paddle attachment, beat on a medium

speed for five minutes. Transfer the mixture to another bowl and thoroughly clean the mixer bowl.

9   Using the cleaned bowl and the whisk attachment, whisk the remaining four egg whites (H, see page 77), adding 30g (1oz) of caster sugar and a pinch of salt (I) until the mixture reaches firm peaks (J).

10   Fold one third of the whisked egg whites into the nut mixture to loosen it using a spatula (K), then gently fold in the rest of the whites (L, M).

11   Divide the mixture evenly between the baking trays (N). Level the mixture with a palette knife so it is 2–3mm ($^1/_{16}$–$^3/_{16}$") deep (O); it should measure approximately 26cm x 34cm (10" x 13½"). Bake for approximately 10 minutes or until golden brown.

12   Remove from the oven and leave to cool for a couple of minutes. Meanwhile, place a sheet of baking parchment on a wire cooling rack.

13   Lift the baked sponge from the tray and place it upside down on the prepared sheet of parchment. Carefully peel the parchment off the back of the sponge and lay it loosely back on top of the sponge. Repeat, layering the next sponge on top of the first sponge and the third sponge on top of that, with a piece of parchment between each. Leave to cool completely.

DARK CHOCOLATE GANACHE

14   Place the chocolate in a bowl. Heat the cream with the orange zest in a saucepan until it just reaches the boil. Pour the cream over the chocolate (P) and stir gently with a whisk until it is all melted and combined (Q). Set aside to cool at room temperature to a spreadable consistency.

ORANGE SYRUP

15   Heat 50ml (1¾fl oz) of water with the sugar in a saucepan, stirring occasionally to ensure all the sugar is dissolved. Bring to the boil.

16   Remove from the heat and add the orange zest and juice. Pour into a jug and leave to cool at room temperature.

ORANGE BUTTERCREAM

17   Combine the egg whites and sugar in the heat-proof bowl of a stand mixer.

18   Place the bowl over a pan of simmering water to create a bain-marie, making sure the water does not touch the bowl. Whisk the mixture (R) until the temperature reaches 60˚C (140°F), or is warm to touch.

19   Fit the bowl onto the stand mixer and beat with a whisk attachment at medium-high speed (S) for eight to 10 minutes until the mixture is thick and shiny.

TOP TIP

The mixture may split initially but don't worry, it will smooth out if you continue whisking.

20   Add the butter a bit at a time, keeping the whisk at a medium speed (T), until it is fully combined. Stir in the orange zest and 2tbsp of juice. Cover and leave at room temperature until required.

CHOCOLATE DECORATIONS

21   Place the transfer sheet on a cool surface (e.g. marble or granite chopping board or worktop) with the rough, cocoa butter side facing upwards.

22   Pour the tempered white chocolate into the middle of the sheet (U) and use a cranked palette knife to spread it over the entire sheet, going over the edges (V, W).

23   Use the tip of a knife to lift the corner of the transfer sheet from the work surface (X), then remove the entire sheet (Y) and leave it on a clean surface to set at room temperature for three to five minutes until touch-dry.

24 Once the chocolate is touch-dry, use a ruler and a sharp knife to trim the edges of the transfer sheet (Z), then cut 10 rectangles from the chocolate measuring approximately 3cm x 9cm (1⅛" x 3½") (AA). Cut each rectangle diagonally to make two right-angled triangles (AB).

TOP TIP

When cutting out the shapes, remember not to cut the transfer sheet; just cut through the chocolate. You will also need to work quickly so you can place the tray on top before the chocolate fully sets.

25 Place the transfer sheet on a flat baking tray, then place another tray on top to keep the chocolate flat. Leave in the refrigerator to set for approximately 20 minutes then remove and leave at room temperature. Peel away the transfer sheet when you are ready to use the decorations (AC).

CRYSTALLISED PISTACHIOS

26 Heat the sugar and 25ml (>¾fl oz) of water in a small saucepan to 119°C (246°F). You may need to tilt the saucepan to get an accurate reading on the thermometer.

27 Once at the right temperature, add the pistachios to the saucepan and stir over the heat until the mixture has a sandy, dry texture.

28 Remove from the heat and turn the nuts onto a tray lined with silicone paper or a heatproof mat. Leave to cool.

ASSEMBLY

29 Once the sponge is cool and all of the components are prepared, the cake can be assembled. Cut each of the sponges in half lengthways. You will need five sponge layers to make up the cake; choose the best-looking one for the top layer.

30 Place the first layer of sponge on a baking tray lined with silicone paper. Brush the cake with orange syrup (AD). Apply an even layer of ganache and smooth it flat with a large palette knife (AE).

31 Place the second layer of sponge on top and brush it with syrup (AF). Apply an even layer of buttercream to the same thickness as the ganache, again smoothing it flat with a large palette knife (AG).

32 Repeat steps 30 and 31 to add the third (AH) and fourth (AI) layers of sponge.

33 Place the fifth and final layer of sponge on top (AJ) and brush it with syrup. Place in the refrigerator, uncovered, to set for approximately two hours.

34 Heat the glaze to 35–40°C (95–105°F). Pour the glaze over the top of the opéra (AK). Smooth it out with a large palette knife if necessary (AL).

TOP TIP

It doesn't matter if the glaze runs over the edges of the opéra as these will be trimmed later.

35 Place the opéra back in the refrigerator, uncovered, for 10 minutes until the glaze has set.

36 Prepare a jug of boiled water, some kitchen paper or a clean tea towel and a serrated knife for cutting the cake.

37 Dip the knife in the hot water then dry it with the kitchen paper. Use the warmed knife to trim and straighten all four sides of the cake (AM). Clean the knife in the hot water and dry it between each cut.

38 Cut slices of cake measuring approximately 3cm x 9cm (1⅛" x 3½") (AN), cleaning the knife between each cut.

39 Use a small palette knife to place the individual slices onto presentation cards or plates. Decorate with the chocolate triangles and crystallised pistachios.

40 Store in the refrigerator for up to two days until ready to serve.

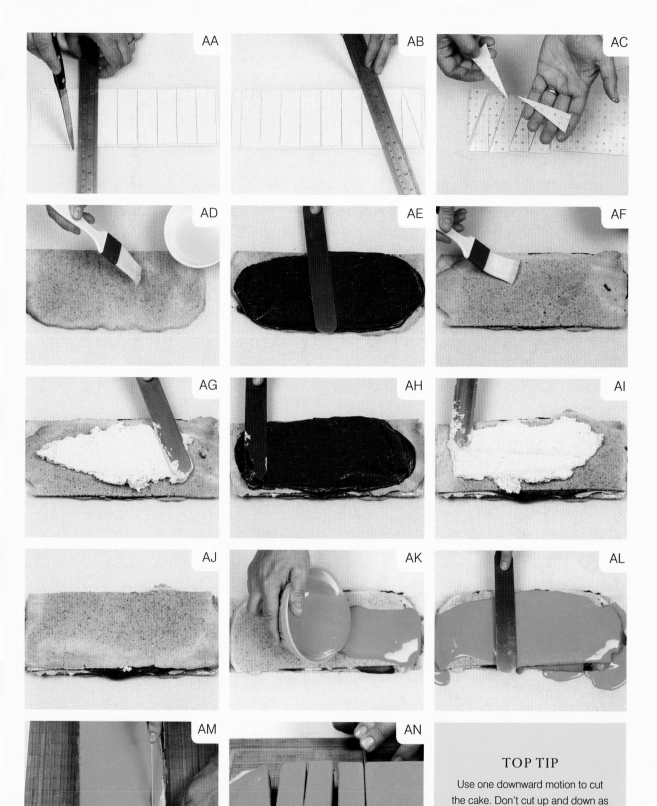

AA

AB

AC

AD

AE

AF

AG

AH

AI

AJ

AK

AL

AM

AN

TOP TIP

Use one downward motion to cut the cake. Don't cut up and down as this will create a messy finish and obscure the layers.

MOUSSE POTS

Complete with chocolate soil and green chocolate leaves, this distinctive dessert is great for dinner parties. It can even be made in advance so there's no rushing around before your guests arrive. I like to use 40% Ghanaian chocolate for the mousse as it has notes of warm caramel and roasted hazelnuts which complement the pears perfectly.

INGREDIENTS

Milk Chocolate Mousse

200ml (7fl oz) whipping cream

45g (1½oz) caster sugar

1 large egg

3 large egg yolks

140g (5oz) milk chocolate

Hazelnut Sponge

1 large egg

65g (2¼oz) icing sugar

65g (2¼oz) ground hazelnuts

10g (¼oz) plain flour

10g (¼oz) unsalted butter, melted

80g (2¾oz) egg whites
(approximately 2 large eggs)

¼tsp cream of tartar

20g (¾oz) caster sugar

Caramelised Pears

700g (1lb 8¾oz) firm pears, peeled,
cored and diced (approximately 4–5
pears, diced weight)

140g (5oz) caster sugar

75ml (2½fl oz) Poire Williams liqueur

1 vanilla pod, seeds only

Chocolate Soil

25g (>¾oz) cocoa powder

35g (1¼oz) plain flour

60g (2oz) ground almonds

60g (2oz) caster sugar

30g (1oz) unsalted butter, melted

Pear Syrup

25g (>¾oz) caster sugar

10ml (¼fl oz) Poire Williams liqueur

Chocolate Green Leaves

200g (7oz) white chocolate,
tempered

1tsp Dark Green dust food colour
(SK)

EQUIPMENT

Basic equipment (see page 18)

40cm x 25cm (16" x 10") acetate
sheet

6–8 glass tumblers: 200–250ml
(7–8¾fl oz) each

Egg tray or muffin tin

38cm x 33cm (15" x 13") baking tray

Circular cutter: just smaller than
circumference of the glasses

MILK CHOCOLATE MOUSSE

1　Whisk the cream to soft peaks.
Store in the refrigerator while you
complete the steps below.

2　Combine the sugar, whole egg
and egg yolks in the heatproof bowl
of a stand mixer. Place the bowl on
a pan of simmering water to create
a bain-marie, making sure the water
doesn't touch the bowl. Whisk the
mixture until it heats to 60°C (140°F)
and the sugar has dissolved.

3　Fit the bowl onto the stand
mixer (A) and beat with the whisk
attachment at a medium speed until
the mixture is light and the bowl has
returned to room temperature (B).

4　Melt the chocolate gently in a
microwave or in a bain-marie until it
reaches approximately 50°C (120°F).

5　Pour the egg mixture into the
melted chocolate and mix them
together vigorously with a whisk (C).
Fold in the whipped cream (D, E).
Transfer the mixture to a large
piping bag.

TOP TIP

When adding the eggs and
sugar to the chocolate, it's
important for the chocolate to
be hot to prevent the mixture
from setting. The mixture may
become stiff and difficult to mix
together but persevere and
it will eventually loosen and
combine.

G

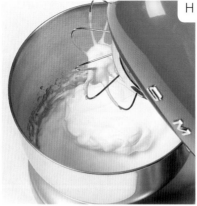

H

I

6   Lay the glasses at a 45° angle on an egg tray. If you don't have an egg tray, put the glasses in a muffin tin and use cling film around the base of each glass to stop it slipping. Pipe the mousse into the glasses, approximately 60g (2oz) per glass so they are one-third full at a diagonal angle (F, see previous page).

7   Place the tray of glasses in the refrigerator overnight.

HAZELNUT SPONGE

8   Preheat the oven to 200°C (400°F/gas mark 6). Line a 38cm x 33cm (15" x 13") baking tray with baking parchment or silicone paper, using cooking oil to stick it to the tray.

9   Use a spatula to stir together the whole egg, icing sugar, ground hazelnuts and flour in a large mixing bowl into a smooth paste (G). Stir the melted butter into the mixture.

10   In a stand mixer fitted with a whisk attachment, whisk the egg whites, cream of tartar and caster sugar at a medium speed for approximately five minutes until it reaches firm peaks (H).

11   Fold one third of the egg whites into the hazelnut paste (I) until fully combined, then gently fold in the remaining egg whites (J).

12   Spread the sponge mixture into a rectangle on the prepared baking tray with a large palette knife to a thickness of approximately 5mm (¼") (K); it should reach to approximately 2cm (¾") from the edge of the tray. Bake for approximately eight to 10 minutes, or until the sponge

is golden. Place a piece of baking parchment on top of a wire cooling rack.

13   Leave to cool on the tray for three minutes. Turn the sponge over onto the wire rack covered with baking parchment, take away the tray and gently peel the baking parchment off the back of the sponge. Lay the removed parchment loosely back on top of the sponge to prevent it from drying out. Leave to cool completely.

CARAMELISED PEARS

14   Peel, core and dice the pears into approximately 5mm (¼") cubes (L).

15   Place a large saucepan on a medium heat and caramelise the sugar a little bit at a time, adding more sugar when the sugar in the pan has dissolved (M–Q).

16   Once all of the sugar has dissolved and reached a caramel colour (R), gradually add the Poire Williams liqueur a little at a time.

17   Add the pears and vanilla seeds and cook on a medium heat for 20–30 minutes or until the caramel liqueur has reduced and become slightly thicker (S). It should look more like a compote. Leave to cool in a bowl at room temperature.

CHOCOLATE SOIL

18   Preheat the oven to 160°C (325°F/gas mark 3).

19   Combine the cocoa powder, flour, ground almonds and sugar in a bowl (T, U, see page 88). Stir the melted butter into the chocolate mixture (V) until it is fully combined (W).

TOP TIPS

The caramel will bubble up a lot when the liqueur is added so be careful as it will be very hot.

Only add more liqueur when the liqueur in the pan is completely combined with the caramel; this will prevent lumps appearing.

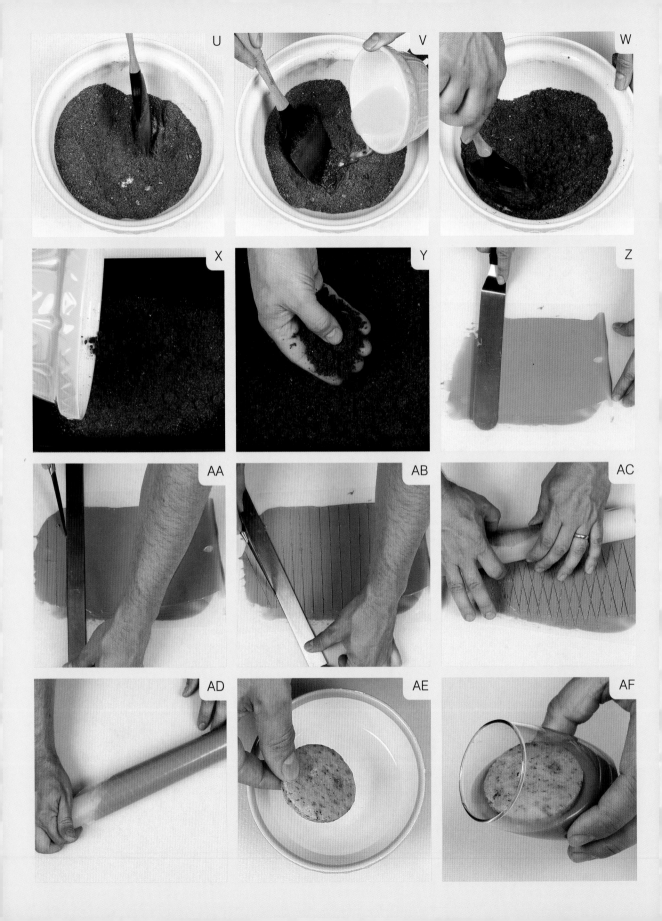

20   Transfer the soil to an unlined baking tray which is at least 3cm (1¹/₈") deep (X) and bake for 20–30 minutes until dry and crumbly.

21   Leave the soil to cool to room temperature in the baking tray, then break up the soil into small pieces with your hand (Y) or blend in a food processor to bring it back to a powder.

PEAR SYRUP

22   Combine the sugar, liqueur and 25ml (>¾fl oz) of water in a saucepan. Bring to the boil whilst stirring. Pour into a small bowl and set aside to cool at room temperature.

GREEN CHOCOLATE LEAVES

23   Add some dark green dust food colour to the tempered chocolate and stir until the desired colour is achieved. The dust will take a minute or so to dissolve into the chocolate.

24   Lay a 40cm x 25cm (16" x 10") sheet of acetate on the work surface or a marble slab. Pour the chocolate onto the sheet and use a palette knife to spread it into an even, thin layer (Z). Leave at room temperature until just touch-dry, approximately three to five minutes.

25   Use a ruler or icing ruler and a sharp knife to cut strips of chocolate across the entire width of the sheet (AA), being careful to cut just the chocolate and not the acetate.

26   Place the ruler at a 45° angle to the vertical lines and cut diagonal strips (AB) to create elongated diamond shapes in the chocolate.

27   Roll up the chocolate onto a rolling pin (AC, AD), secure it with a little tape then slide out the rolling pin. Place the chocolate in the refrigerator to set for approximately 20 minutes.

ASSEMBLY

28   Cut out a disc of hazelnut sponge for each of the mousses. The diameter of the disc should be the same size as or slightly smaller than the diameter of your glass. Dip each disc of sponge into the bowl of syrup (AE), turning it over quickly so both sides are coated without being soaked, then place them on top of the mousse in the glasses (AF).

29   Strain any excess liquid from the caramelised pears. Spoon them into the glass (AG), holding the glass tilted at first and gradually righting it until the layer of pears reaches 2cm (¾") from the top of the glass. Top with a layer of chocolate soil (AH).

30   Unroll the green chocolate sheet close to the work surface; the chocolate leaves should fall away (AI). Finish the chocolate pots by planting three chocolate leaves in the middle of each glass.

31   Store in the refrigerator for up to two days until ready to serve.

WHITE CHOCOLATE
PANNA COTTA

This is my take on the classic peaches and cream combination, with the rosemary adding flavour complexity and a splash of colour. It's an easy and impressive dessert for dinner parties – if you're short of time, omit the chocolate decorations.

INGREDIENTS

Panna Cotta

2 sheets of leaf gelatine

65ml (2¼fl oz) semi-skimmed milk

1tsp vanilla paste

65g (2¼oz) white chocolate

300ml (10½fl oz) whipping cream

Decorations

300g (10½oz) white chocolate, tempered

4 sugar flowers (optional)

Roasted Peaches

6 sprigs fresh rosemary

35g (1¼oz) soft brown sugar

100ml (3½fl oz) peach schnapps

½tsp vanilla paste

2 fresh peaches

EQUIPMENT

Basic equipment (see page 18)

4 martini glasses

Acetate sheet: large enough to fit four of the biggest circles

3 circular cake cards or circular cutters: 1 x the same size as the martini glass rim, 1 x 1cm (³/₈") larger and 1 x 1cm (³/₈") smaller

Griddle pan

MAKES 4 DESSERTS

PANNA COTTA

1   Soak the gelatine in just enough cold water to cover the leaves for five minutes, until it has softened.

2   Place the milk and vanilla paste in a saucepan (A) and bring to the boil. Squeeze the water out of the soaked gelatine then add the gelatine to the pan (B). Turn off the heat and stir continuously until the gelatine has dissolved (C).

3   Add the white chocolate (D) and stir until melted (E). Stir in the cream (F) and, once it is all combined, pour the mixture into a jug. Set aside for five to 10 minutes at room temperature to cool slightly.

4   Pour the mixture into four martini glasses (G) and leave in the refrigerator to set for one hour, or overnight at the longest. If you leave them for longer, the surface can dry out and harden.

TOP TIP

It can be difficult to move the martini glasses once filled so put the glasses in the refrigerator before pouring the mixture into them.

CHOCOLATE DECORATIONS

5   Spread an even layer of tempered white chocolate, approximately 2mm (¹/₁₆") thick, onto a sheet of acetate using a large palette knife (H).

6   Leave to set for three to five minutes until just touch-dry. Working quickly, place the largest cake card, foil side down, on the chocolate and use a sharp knife to cut out a circle (I). Alternatively, use a circular cutter. Replace with the next size down, ensuring it is placed directly in the centre, and cut another circle. Cut out a third circle using the same method with the smallest card (J). Repeat to cut out circles for the remaining three glasses.

7   Place all of the rings on a baking tray lined with a clean sheet of acetate or silicone paper. Cover with another piece of acetate or silicone paper and lay another tray on top to keep them flat. Place in the refrigerator to chill for at least 20 minutes and up to one hour.

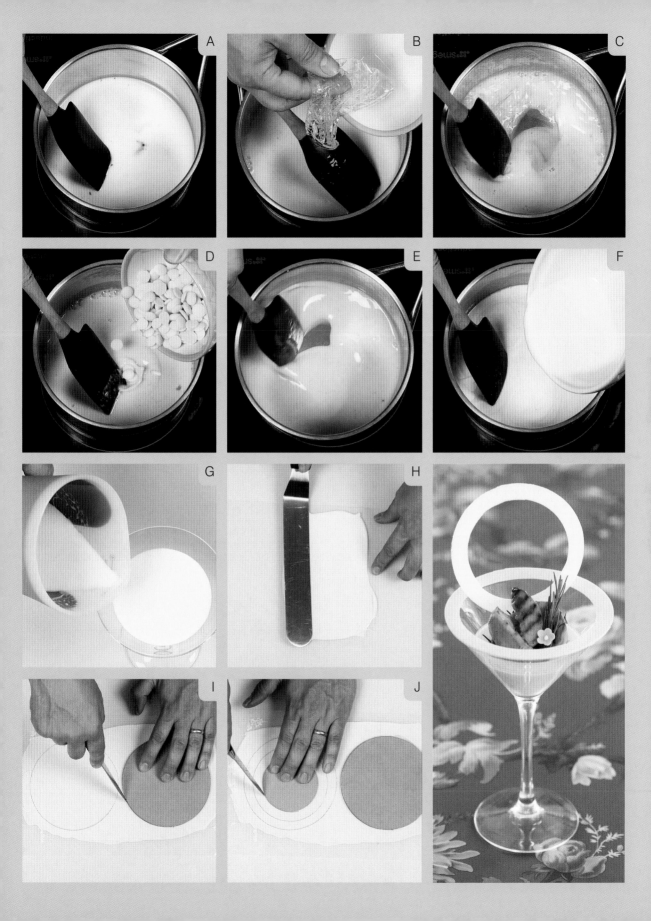

ROASTED PEACHES

8 Remove the leaves from two sprigs of rosemary and put them in a large bowl along with the sugar, schnapps and vanilla paste and stir to combine.

9 Cut the peaches into eighths and place them in the bowl, discarding the stone. Stir the peaches gently to coat them with the schnapps mixture, being careful to not break up the fruit. Place in the refrigerator for one hour.

10 Heat up a griddle pan then place the peaches on top (K). Cook on each side for approximately four to six minutes until slightly softened and lightly charred (L). Brush a little of the remaining syrup onto the peaches as they cook. Set aside to cool slightly to serve them warm, or leave to cool completely.

TO SERVE

11 Remove the panna cottas from the refrigerator just before serving. Place the peaches on top. Place the larger chocolate rings on the rims of the glasses and the smaller ones inside at an angle.

12 Decorate each dessert with a sprig of rosemary and, if serving with cooled peaches, add a sugar flower.

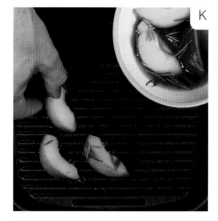

MOCHA
ÉCLAIRS

Rich chocolate and roasted coffee is one of my favourite pairings. Handmade cigarillos elevate these éclairs to pâtisserie window status, and once you have learnt the technique you can use cigarillos to decorate all manner of chocolate treats, from adorning individual desserts to surrounding entire cake tiers.

INGREDIENTS

Choux Pastry

120ml (4¼fl oz) milk

100g (3½oz) unsalted butter, cubed

2 pinches of salt

2 pinches of sugar

100g (3½oz) plain flour

40g (1¾oz) cocoa powder

4–5 large eggs, beaten

Mocha Cream

100ml (3½fl oz) milk

3tbsp instant coffee

80g (2¾oz) egg yolks (approximately 4 large egg yolks)

40g (1½oz) caster sugar

250g (8¾oz) milk chocolate, chopped or in callets

250ml (8¾fl oz) whipping cream

Cigarillos

200g (7oz) white chocolate

1tsp finely ground coffee

Gold Coffee Beans

25 coffee beans

½tsp Gold dust food colour (SK)

EQUIPMENT

Basic equipment (see page 18)

Piping nozzles: 1.5cm (½") open star and 2cm (¾") petal

Spray bottle for water

MAKES 20–25 ÉCLAIRS

CHOCOLATE CHOUX PASTRY

1 Preheat the oven to 175°C (345°F/gas mark 5). Place 130ml (4½fl oz) of water with the milk, butter, salt and sugar in a large saucepan on a medium heat and bring it to the boil, stirring occasionally (A). Meanwhile, sift the flour and cocoa powder into a bowl.

2 Remove from the heat and add the flour and cocoa powder all at once, stirring quickly and vigorously to combine (B).

3 Return to the hob and continue stirring over a medium heat for up to five minutes until the paste starts to break up slightly and becomes almost crumbly (C).

4 Remove from the heat and transfer to a freestanding mixer fitted with the paddle beater attachment. Beat the mixture at a slow speed for a couple of minutes to cool slightly then gradually add the eggs a little at a time (D). Continue adding the eggs until it becomes a smooth, shiny paste (E). You may not need to add all of the eggs. The consistency of the paste should not be runny; it should slowly drop off a spoon, leaving a smooth 'V' shape.

5 Fill a large piping bag fitted with a star nozzle with the mixture. Line a baking tray with a baking mat or silicone paper.

6 Pipe lines of the mixture approximately 12cm (5") long diagonally from the corner of the tray (F), making sure that they are even in length and thickness.

7 Spray with water and place in the preheated oven for 15 minutes, then reduce the heat to 160°C (325°F/gas mark 3) for a further 10–15 minutes, until crisp. Leave to cool in the oven with the door slightly open for 10–15 minutes. Remove from the oven and allow to cool fully; the éclairs can be frozen at this point for up to three months in an airtight container.

MOCHA CREAM

8 Place the milk and coffee in a saucepan (G) and bring to the boil, stirring occasionally. Meanwhile, whisk the egg yolks and sugar together in a bowl.

9 Pour the hot coffee milk into the yolk mixture (H). Return it to the saucepan and heat on low, whisking continuously for two to three minutes until the mixture thickens (I).

10 Place the chocolate in a medium bowl and pour the hot mixture over it (J). Leave it to stand for two minutes then whisk together (K) until the chocolate has melted and is fully incorporated.

11 Whip the cream to soft-peak consistency, then whisk one third of it into the chocolate mixture (L). Once combined, whisk in the rest of the cream (M) and place it in the refrigerator for a minimum of two hours or, ideally, overnight.

> **TOP TIP**
>
> Mix in one third of the cream first to bring down the temperature of the hot mixture before mixing in the rest; if you fold it all in at once, the cream can split.

CIGARILLOS

12 Temper the white chocolate then stir in the finely ground coffee.

13 Use a large palette knife to spread a small amount of the chocolate onto a marble or granite slab. Spread it from one side to the other continuously (N), into an even layer, until the chocolate sets. Leave for three to five minutes or until just touch-dry.

14 Hold a large chocolate scraper at an acute angle close to the chocolate and use it to scrape away the edges of the chocolate with some force to create a neat rectangle (O, P).

15 Position the marble or granite slab so that you are facing one of the shorter sides of the rectangle. Place the edge of the chocolate scraper approximately 6cm ($2^3/_8$") down from the furthest end of the chocolate. Push the scraper away from you to scrape and lift the chocolate into a curl to the end of the rectangle (Q). Repeat to make 25 cigarillos.

GOLD COFFEE BEANS

16 Place the coffee beans in a small bowl and add the gold dust food colour (R). Shake the bowl until the beans are all covered in gold.

17 Transfer the beans to a piece of kitchen paper, lift it at the sides and shake the beans around to remove the excess dust food colour (S).

ASSEMBLY

18 Slice off the very top edge of the éclairs with a serrated knife (T). Fill a large piping bag with half of the mocha cream and snip off the end; use this to fill the éclairs (U).

19 Place the remaining cream in another piping bag fitted with a 2cm ($^3/_4$") petal nozzle and pipe from side to side down the length of each éclair (V).

20 Place a cigarillo on top of the cream (W) and add a dusted cocoa bean towards one end.

21 Store the éclairs in an airtight container in the refrigerator for up to two days.

HAZELNUT, GINGER & CARAMEL
CHOCOLATE DOMES

I teach a variation of this recipe as part of my French Pâtisserie course at Squires Kitchen International School. Once you perfect the shiny chocolate glaze, the domes really are exquisite and taste as good as they look. In the chocolate mousse I like to use a combination of 67% Madagascan dark chocolate and 39% Ecuadorian Arriba milk chocolate, which both have an intense cocoa flavour with hints of fruit to complement the hazelnut and ginger.

INGREDIENTS

Ginger Brûlée

115ml (4fl oz) whipping cream

45ml (1½fl oz) semi-skimmed milk

12g (½oz) fresh ginger, grated

2 large egg yolks

30g (1oz) caster sugar

Hazelnut Sponge

50g (1¾oz) icing sugar

50g (1¾oz) ground hazelnuts

40g (1½oz) whole eggs
(approximately 1 medium egg)

30g (1oz) egg yolks (approximately
2 medium eggs)

95g (3¼oz) egg whites
(approximately 3 medium eggs)

35g (1¼oz) caster sugar

Pinch of salt

45g (1½oz) plain flour, sifted

30g (1oz) unsalted butter, melted

Hazelnut Praline

250g (8¾oz) blanched hazelnuts

180g (6¼oz) caster sugar

Caramel and Chocolate Mousse

50g (1¾oz) caster sugar

270ml (9½fl oz) whipping cream

5g (<¼oz) liquid glucose

100g (3½oz) dark chocolate,
chopped or in callets

35g (1¼oz) milk chocolate,
chopped or in callets

Chocolate Leaves

100g (3½oz) dark chocolate,
tempered

Chocolate Glaze

12g (½oz) powdered gelatine

100ml (3½fl oz) whipping cream

150g (5¼oz) caster sugar

75g (2½oz) liquid glucose

50g (1¾oz) cocoa powder, sifted

Decoration

1 sheet of edible gold leaf

EQUIPMENT

Basic equipment (see page 18)

5.5cm (2¼") circular cutter

Half-sphere silicone moulds: 1 x
3cm and 2 x 7cm (1 x 1⅛" and 2 x
2¾") (Silikomart)

10cm (4") wide acetate strip

7cm (2¾") tube

12 circular presentation cards:
7.5cm (3")

MAKES 10–12 DOMES

GINGER BRÛLÉE

1   Preheat the oven to 110°C (225°F/
gas mark ¼).

2   Heat the cream, milk and ginger
in a saucepan to just before it reaches
the boil. Remove from the heat and
leave to cool for five minutes.

3   Whisk the egg yolks and
sugar together in a small bowl for
approximately five minutes until the
mixture turns pale and thick.

4   Pour half of the hot cream into
the egg mixture (A) and whisk until
combined (B). Pour the egg mixture
into the saucepan (C), whisk to
combine with the remaining cream
and return to a low heat for one
minute (D).

5   Sieve the brûlée mixture into a
bowl to remove the ginger (E), using
a whisk or the back of a soup ladle
to help push the mixture through.
Transfer half of the mixture to a jug.

TOP TIP

This ginger brûlée recipe makes
double the amount needed
as it's hard to make a smaller
amount. You can freeze any
remaining mixture for up to a
month for use at a later date.

6   Place the 3cm (1⅛") half-sphere
silicone mould in a shallow baking
tray. Fill to 2mm (1/16") from the top
of the half spheres with the brûlée
mixture (F).

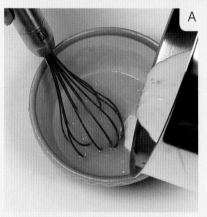

A

B

C

D

E

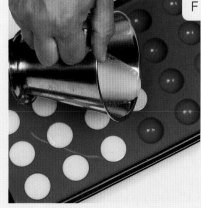

F

7   Carefully place the tray in the preheated oven then add some hot, boiled water to a depth of 1cm ($^3/_8$") underneath the mould. Bake for one hour or until the brûlées have set but are still wobbly.

8   Leave to cool to room temperature for approximately 30 minutes, then place in the freezer for two hours until fully set and frozen.

HAZELNUT SPONGE

9   Preheat the oven to 190°C (375°F/ gas mark 5). Line a baking tray with silicone paper.

10   Place the icing sugar, ground hazelnuts, whole eggs and egg yolks in a mixing bowl and use a spatula to beat it into a paste.

11   In a freestanding mixer fitted with a whisk attachment, whisk the egg whites (G) to soft peaks. Add the caster sugar and salt (H) and whisk on a high speed until it reaches stiff peaks to create a meringue.

12   Beat a third of the meringue into the nut paste to loosen it. Fold in the rest of the meringue as lightly as possible (I). Fold in the flour and, before the mixture is fully blended, add the melted butter (J). Continue to fold lightly until fully combined.

13   Pour the mixture onto the lined baking tray and gently spread it into a smooth, even layer (K). Bake in the preheated oven for 10–15 minutes or until the sponge is golden (L). Place a piece of baking parchment on top of a wire cooling rack.

14   Leave to cool on the tray for three minutes. Turn the cake over onto the wire rack covered with baking parchment, take away the tray and gently peel the baking parchment off the back of the sponge (M). Lay the removed parchment loosely back on top of the sponge to prevent it from drying out. Set aside to cool for approximately 20 minutes.

TOP TIP

The sponge can be frozen at this stage for up to three months. Wrap well with cling film and freeze it flat. Approximately two hours before needed, defrost the sponge at room temperature, still keeping it wrapped in cling film.

15   Use a circular cutter to cut out 10–12 5.5cm (2¼") discs of sponge.

HAZELNUT PRALINE

16   Roast the hazelnuts in the oven at 160°C (325°F/ gas mark 3) for five to 10 minutes until golden. Roughly chop the hazelnuts (N, O) and line a baking tray with silicone paper or a silicone baking mat.

17   Heat the sugar and 50ml (1¾fl oz) of water in a medium saucepan to 119°C (246°F). Add the roasted hazelnuts while they are still warm, stirring continuously (P).

18   The sugar and water will take on a sandy texture (Q); keep the pan on a medium heat until the sugar returns to a liquid caramel (R). Take the saucepan off the heat and pour the caramelised nuts onto the lined baking tray. Set aside to cool at room temperature for 30 minutes.

19   Once cold, separate the nuts with a knife then place the praline in an airtight container.

CARAMEL AND CHOCOLATE MOUSSE

20 Heat the sugar in a saucepan over a medium heat until it becomes a golden caramel: stir gently with a wooden spoon only when the sugar starts to caramelise (S).

21 Heat 100ml (3½fl oz) of whipping cream in a small bowl in the microwave until just before it boils. Add it to the caramel a little at a time (T), stirring very well to deglaze the pan (U). Continue to add the cream a little at a time until fully incorporated. Stir in the glucose.

TOP TIP

It's important to add the cream in very small quantities and stir vigorously in between each addition as it prevents crystal lumps from forming. If lumps do form, sieve the caramel as you pour it over the chocolate to remove them.

22 Place the chocolates in a bowl. Pour the caramel over the top (V) and stir until all the chocolate has melted (W). Leave to cool at room temperature, until warm but not cold.

23 Whisk the remaining 170ml (5¾fl oz) of cream to soft peaks, then fold it into the warm chocolate mixture a third at a time to prevent the chocolate mixture from setting and creating lumps (X, Y).

24 Transfer the mixture to a piping bag until needed or use immediately.

DOME PREPARATION

25   Place the 7cm (2¾") half-sphere moulds on baking trays. Pipe a little chocolate mousse into each cavity (Z).

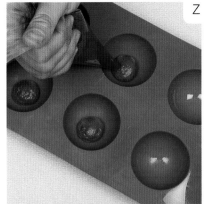
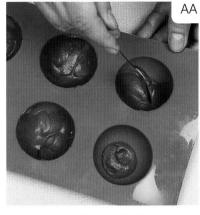

26   Use a small spoon with an upward motion to press the mousse up against the sides of the mould, covering the entire surface of each half sphere and removing any air bubbles to ensure a smooth finish when the mousse is demoulded (AA).

27   Pipe a disc of mousse into the centre of each half sphere, approximately one third of the depth of the mould (AB). Place a frozen brûlée on top, with the flat edge facing upwards. Push each brûlée down a little, but don't let it touch the bottom of the mould (AC).

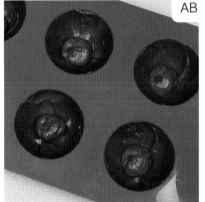
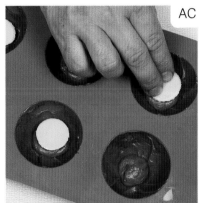

28   Pipe more mousse into each half sphere, first around the sides of the brûlée and then on top so it is completely encased (AD).

29   Sprinkle some hazelnut praline into each half sphere, then pipe in a little more mousse until it reaches 5mm (¼") from the top edge (AE).

30   Place a disc of hazelnut sponge on top of the mousse in the centre of each half sphere and press it down gently (AF).

31   Pipe in more mousse around the edge if needed. Level and remove any excess mousse with a small palette knife (AG). Place in the freezer for at least four hours or, ideally, overnight.

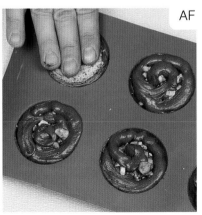

CHOCOLATE LEAVES

TOP TIP

If you lightly oil the slab beforehand it will help the acetate to stick, making it easier to lift the knife.

32   Place a strip of acetate on a marble or granite slab. Dip the blade of a small, sharp, pointed knife halfway into the tempered dark chocolate (AH).

33   Hold the acetate down with your free hand and press the chocolate-coated knife down flat, about 2.5cm (1") from the edge of the sheet (AI). Angle the knife so just the tip is touching the chocolate and draw it towards you to create a central vein and a short stem at the end of the leaf (AJ).

34   Repeat to make 12 leaves in total, using another piece of acetate if required. Slide the acetate into a tube to give the leaves a curve (AK). Leave to set at room temperature for three to five minutes until touch-dry, then place in the refrigerator for 10–15 minutes.

CHOCOLATE GLAZE

35   Add 70ml (2½fl oz) of water to the gelatine in a small bowl, stirring to ensure it is well combined. Set aside for approximately five minutes until all the water is absorbed.

36   Combine the cream, sugar, glucose, cocoa powder and 75ml (2½fl oz) of water in a saucepan and boil until the mixture reaches 106°C (223°F) (AL). Remove from the heat and transfer to a bowl to cool slightly.

37   Once the glaze has cooled to 70°C (158°F), add the soaked gelatine (AM). Stir with a whisk until dissolved and fully combined (AN).

38   Pour the glaze into a jug, passing it through a sieve to remove any lumps. Cover with cling film touching the surface of the glaze and leave to cool at room temperature until required.

TOP TIP

The glaze can be frozen at this point for up to three months. When needed, defrost overnight in the refrigerator then heat to pouring temperature following the steps below.

ASSEMBLY

39   The optimum pouring temperature for the glaze is 35–40°C (95–105°F). If necessary, reheat the glaze gently before use. Place a small cranked palette knife in a cup of hot, boiled water. Have the presentation cards ready to use and place a wire rack over a sided baking tray.

40   Remove the half spheres from the freezer. Remove them from the moulds by pushing the silicone half spheres up from underneath; the mousses should be released as the mould is inverted (AO). Place them on the wire rack.

41   Whilst the glaze is at the correct temperature, pour it over one mousse at a time (AP). Check that each one is completely covered before moving on to the next and work quickly to ensure a smooth finish. Don't be tempted to pour another layer of glaze if you find a spot you've missed as it won't achieve a smooth finish.

42   Remove each mousse from the wire rack as quickly as possible: take the palette knife from the hot water and, without drying it, slide it under the glazed mousse. While still on the rack, gently move the palette knife around the circumference of the half sphere to smooth any drips at the bottom edge (AQ). Lift the mousse and place it on a presentation card (AR). Dip the palette knife into the water between releasing each mousse: this reheats the knife and removes excess chocolate which could stick to the next mousse when it is being placed on the card.

43   While the glaze is still wet, gently press hazelnut praline around the bottom edge of each mousse (AS). Place a chocolate leaf on top with a little more praline. Add a touch of gold leaf to finish. Store in the refrigerator for up to two days.

CUT & SHARE

BLACKBERRY, LIME & CHOCOLATE
ENTREMETS

An entremets is a dessert made up of layers and surrounded by mousse. The whole cake is then finished with a high-gloss glaze or sprayed with cocoa butter after being frozen. A version of this recipe helped me win the UK Chocolate Masters in 2009 so it's a huge favourite of mine. I like to use 67% Madagascan chocolate for the brownie and chocolate mousse because it has a clear, rounded cocoa flavour and notes of raspberries and bilberries which complement the blackberries.

INGREDIENTS

Chocolate Glaze

3 sheets of leaf gelatine

75g (2½oz) liquid glucose

75g (2½oz) caster sugar

50g (1¾oz) condensed milk

75g (2½oz) white chocolate, chopped or in callets

Dust food colours: 2tsp Edelweiss, ½tsp Fern and 2tsp Violet (SK)

Brownie

15g (½oz) unsalted butter

40g (1½oz) light brown sugar

10g (¼oz) golden syrup

15g (½oz) plain flour

1 medium egg

45g (1½oz) dark chocolate, chopped or in callets

15g (½oz) blanched almonds, roasted and roughly chopped

10g (¼oz) cocoa nibs

Blackberry Purée

50g (1¾oz) caster sugar

500g (1lb 1¾oz) blackberries

2tsp lemon juice

Blackberry Cream

½ a sheet of leaf gelatine

100g (3½oz) blackberry purée

40g (1½oz) whole egg (approximately 1 medium egg)

30g (1oz) egg yolks (approximately 2 medium eggs)

25g (>¾oz) caster sugar

20g (¾oz) unsalted butter, cubed

SERVES 8–10

Lime Panna Cotta

1 sheet of leaf gelatine

30ml (1fl oz) lime juice (1–2 limes)

1 lime, zest

½ vanilla pod, seeds only

30g (1oz) white chocolate, chopped or in callets

160ml (5½fl oz) whipping cream

Chocolate Mousse

250ml (8¾fl oz) whipping cream

25g (>¾oz) caster sugar

50g (1¾oz) egg yolks (approximately 3 medium eggs)

125g (4½oz) dark chocolate, chopped or in callets

Chocolate Decorations

200g (7oz) white chocolate, tempered

2tsp Fern dust food colour (SK)

Garnish

5 fresh blackberries

2tsp Silver dust food colour (SK)

3 edible purple pansies

EQUIPMENT

Basic equipment (see page 18)

15cm (6") round, loose-bottomed sandwich tin

18cm (7") round, 4.5cm (1¾") deep pâtisserie ring

Acetate strips: 1cm x 60cm (³/₈" x 23²/₃") and 5cm x 60cm (2" x 23²/₃")

Cook's blowtorch

20.5cm (8") cake board

CHOCOLATE GLAZE

1 Soak the gelatine in 30ml (1fl oz) of water for 10 minutes.

2 Place 35ml (1¼fl oz) of water with the glucose, sugar and condensed milk in a saucepan and heat to 103°C (217°F). Remove from the heat.

3 Add the soaked gelatine and any leftover water. Use a hand blender to blend the mixture.

4 Add the white chocolate and blend until melted. Add 2tsp of white dust food colour and blend again until fully incorporated.

5 Colour 25ml (>¾fl oz) of the glaze with ½tsp of lime green dust food colour. Colour the remaining glaze with 2tsp of purple dust food colour.

6 Pour the glazes through a fine sieve into airtight containers. Place in the refrigerator to set overnight.

BROWNIE

7 Grease and line the bottom of a 15cm (6") sandwich tin with a disc of silicone paper (A). Preheat the oven to 170°C (340°F/gas mark 3).

8 Beat the butter, sugar, golden syrup and flour in a stand mixer fitted with a paddle attachment until fully combined. Add the egg (B) and beat until fully combined.

9 Meanwhile, melt the chocolate in the microwave or a bain-marie. Once it has cooled slightly, add the chocolate to the cake mixture (C).

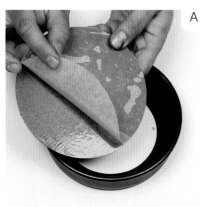

A

B

C

Stir in the almonds and cocoa nibs with a spatula (D).

10 Pour the mixture into the prepared tin (E, F) and bake for 20 minutes, until a crust has formed on top but it is still soft in middle. Leave to cool at room temperature.

BLACKBERRY PURÉE

11 Heat 50ml (1¾fl oz) of water with the sugar into a small pan, stirring occasionally to dissolve the sugar. Bring to the boil then add the blackberries and simmer for five minutes, stirring occasionally. Remove from the heat and blend in a food processor.

12 Pass the purée through a fine sieve into a bowl. Use the back of a soup ladle to extract as much of the juice and pulp as possible. Scrape the underside of the sieve to capture all of the purée. Add the lemon juice. Cover the bowl with cling film and set aside to cool until required.

BLACKBERRY CREAM

13 Lightly grease and line a 15cm (6") sandwich tin as in step 7. Soak the gelatine for five to 10 minutes in enough cold water to cover it.

14 Heat the blackberry pureé in a saucepan (G), whisking occasionally, and bring to the boil. Meanwhile, whisk the whole eggs, yolks and sugar together in a small bowl.

15 Pour the pureé into the egg mixture (H) and whisk until fully combined (I). Return the mixture to the saucepan to thicken, stirring over a low heat for approximately one minute (J).

16 Squeeze out the excess water from the gelatine then whisk it in (K) until it has all dissolved. Add the butter (L) and whisk until fully incorporated.

17 Pour into the prepared tin (M, N) and place in the freezer for at least 30 minutes or until required.

LIME PANNA COTTA

TOP TIP

There is no sugar added to this panna cotta; white chocolate provides the sweetness.

18 Soak the gelatine for five to 10 minutes in enough cold water to cover it.

19 Place the lime juice, zest and vanilla seeds in a small saucepan and cook on a low heat until boiling (O). Remove from the heat.

20 Squeeze the excess water from the gelatine and whisk it into the hot juice mixture (P) until dissolved. Add the white chocolate (Q) and stir until melted. Pour in the cream (R) and whisk until fully incorporated.

21 Pour the mixture on top of the frozen blackberry cream in the sandwich tin and return to the freezer to set, approximately one hour or until required.

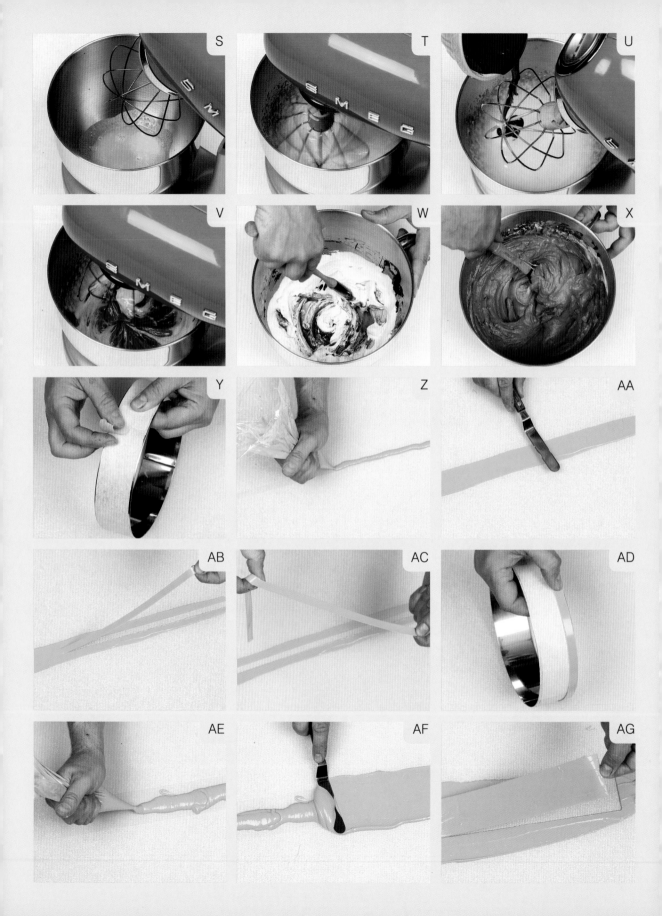

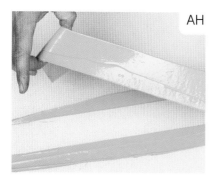

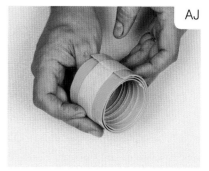

CHOCOLATE MOUSSE

22 Whip the cream to soft peaks. Meanwhile, boil 25ml (>¾fl oz) of water and pour it into a small bowl with the sugar, stirring until dissolved.

23 Transfer the dissolved sugar to a stand mixer fitted with a whisk attachment. Add the egg yolks (S) and whisk until light and fluffy (T).

24 Melt the chocolate in a microwave or a bain-marie and pour it into the mixture (U). Whisk (V) until fully incorporated.

25 Remove the bowl from the mixer and fold in the cream by hand (W, X). Cover and leave at room temperature until ready to use.

CHOCOLATE DECORATIONS

26 Colour the white chocolate with 2tsp of lime green dust food colour and transfer to a large piping bag.

27 Wrap a 4.5cm x 51cm (1¾" x 20") strip of silicone paper around the outside of an 18cm (7") pâtisserie ring and secure at the join with a little tape on the top edge (Y). Snip off the end of the bag of lime green chocolate.

28 Pipe the chocolate on top of the 1cm x 60cm (³⁄₈" x 23²⁄₃") strip of acetate (Z) then use a palette knife to spread it into an even, thin layer over the edges of the acetate (AA).

29 Pick up the acetate from one end (AB) and use your fingers to smooth the edges to ensure they are straight (AC).

30 Leave on a clean, flat work surface at room temperature for three to five minutes, until the chocolate has a matt surface.

31 Place the 18cm (7") pâtisserie ring on a tray or cake board. Wrap the chocolate-coated acetate around the bottom edge of the outside of the ring so the chocolate faces inwards. Pinch the ends of the strip together where they meet (AD) then place in the refrigerator for 15 minutes to set.

32 Repeat steps 28 and 29 with the 5cm x 60cm (2" x 23²⁄₃") strip of acetate (AE–AH). As the chocolate sets, use a craft knife and a ruler to cut lots of thin strips in different widths from the chocolate (AI).

33 Before the chocolate sets completely, roll the acetate sheet around the end of a rolling pin with the chocolate facing inwards. Secure the roll with some masking tape then slide the acetate off the end of the rolling pin (AJ). Leave in the refrigerator to set for 15 minutes.

ASSEMBLY

TOP TIP

The most important thing to remember when making an entremets is to make sure that the layering is level and central. The inserts also need to be well frozen, if the recipe calls for it, and the completed cake needs to be well frozen before it is sprayed or glazed.

34 Line a 20.5cm (8") cake board with some silicone paper. Place the brownie in the centre of the lined board.

35 Remove the frozen blackberry cream and lime panna cotta disc from the tin: I find it helps to use a blowtorch or a warm cloth to heat the side of the tin briefly. If it has softened, place it back in the freezer for 10 minutes. Place the disc on top of the brownie (AK), using a little chocolate mousse between the layers to help them stick together.

36 Place the 18cm (7") pâtisserie ring around the entremets fillings, ensuring that they are in the centre of the ring. Transfer half of the mousse to a large piping bag, snip off the end and pipe into the gap around the edge of the brownie (AL).

37 Use a palette knife to spread the mousse up the sides of the ring to prevent air bubbles from forming around the edge (AM).

38 Spread more mousse on top of the fillings. Use a large palette knife to smooth the top and scrape it off so the mousse is level with the top edge of the pâtisserie ring (AN). Place in the freezer for approximately two hours to freeze completely. If the top becomes concave, add some more mousse to level it out and place back in the freezer.

39 Heat the two glazes to 35–40°C (95–105°F). Pour the purple glaze into a jug and transfer the green glaze to a piping bag.

40 Remove the filled mousse from the freezer. Take it off the cake board and place it on top of a bowl with a smaller circumference (AO). Use a blowtorch to heat the side of the ring briefly to release it from the mousse (AP), then remove it by pushing the ring down (AQ). Place the filled mousse back on the cake board and put it back in the freezer for two minutes or until ready to glaze.

41 Take the mousse off the cake board and place it on a wire rack with a sided baking tray underneath.

42 Pour all of the purple glaze over the top of the mousse (AR). Use the back of a metal spoon to spread the glaze so it covers the sides of the mousse as well as the top (AS). Use the long edge of a large palette knife to lightly scrape the top to create a smooth, even finish, without pulling away too much of the glaze (AT). Place the blade of the palette knife in a jug of hot, boiled water.

43 Immediately pipe lines of green glaze over one side of the cake (AU). Leave the entremets on the wire rack until it stops dripping, then hold the underside of the entremets with your fingertips and use the wet palette knife to gently wipe the drips onto the underside of the entremets.

44 Wet the palette knife again and use it to help place the entremets in the centre of a clean cake board or serving plate. Slide the palette knife out; the water should help it come away easily.

45 If the entremets is not immediately required it can now be frozen in an airtight container for up to one month: ensure you don't cover over the glaze with cling film or foil as this will spoil the finish. Alternatively, it can be kept in the fridge to fully defrost for approximately four hours, or up to two days, before serving.

46 When ready to serve, carefully remove the acetate from the green chocolate decorations (AV). Place the large ring around the edge of the entremets and break up the small rings to decorate the top of the cake. Garnish with some blackberries dusted with silver dust food colour and fresh purple pansies.

TOP TIP

When cutting an entremets, it is best to use a hot knife. Fill a jug with hot, boiled water and place the blade of a large, sharp carving knife into it for a minute. Dry the knife with kitchen paper before cutting and repeat between each cut.

CHOCOLATE

I love making entremets because you can use so many different flavour combinations and finishes to create something new and exciting. I enjoy taking a recipe I already have, adding new elements and choosing how to present it to give a hint of what's inside. This recipe would also work well with lime in place of lemon.

INGREDIENTS

Pink and White Chocolate Glazes

3 sheets of leaf gelatine

75g (2½oz) caster sugar

75g (2½oz) liquid glucose

50g (1¾oz) condensed milk

75g (2½oz) white chocolate

Dust food colours: 2tsp Extra White and 2tsp Pink (SK)

Almond Sponge

45g (1½oz) ground almonds

10g (¼oz) plain flour

10g (¼oz) unsalted butter, melted

1 large egg

2 large eggs, separated

70g (2½oz) caster sugar

Raspberry Cream

2 sheets of leaf gelatine

110g (3¾oz) raspberry pureé

70g (2½oz) egg yolks (approximately 4 large eggs)

35g (1¼oz) caster sugar

35g (1¼oz) unsalted butter, cubed

Raspberry Jelly

2 sheets of leaf gelatine

100g (3½oz) raspberry pureé

35g (1¼oz) caster sugar

5g (<¼oz) cornflour

White Chocolate and Lemon Mousse

370ml (13fl oz) whipping cream

100g (3½oz) white chocolate, chopped or in callets

35g (1¼oz) egg yolks (approximately 2 large egg yolks)

20g (¾oz) caster sugar

15g (½oz) custard powder

30g (1oz) powdered cocoa butter (SK)

2tbsp lemon juice (approximately 1 lemon)

1 lemon, zest

Decorations

100g (3½oz) white chocolate, tempered

5 fresh raspberries

Silver dust food colour (SK)

1 lemon

EQUIPMENT

Basic equipment (see page 18)

Circular cutters: 3cm, 4cm, 5cm, 9cm and 15cm (1⅛", 1½", 2", 3½"and 6")

Acetate sheets: 2 x 25cm x 40cm (10" x 16")

15cm (6") round, loose-bottomed sandwich tin

9cm (3½") pâtisserie ring

18cm (7") savarin silicone mould

Cook's blow torch

38cm x 33cm (15" x 13") baking tray

SERVES 8–10

PINK AND WHITE CHOCOLATE GLAZES

1 Soak the gelatine in 30ml (1fl oz) of water for 10 minutes.

2 Heat 35ml (1¼fl oz) of water with the sugar, glucose and condensed milk in a saucepan to 103°C (217°F).

3 Add the soaked gelatine and any remaining water. Use a hand blender to blend the mixture.

4 Add the white chocolate and blend until melted. Divide the mixture in half: colour one half with the pink dust food colour and the other half with the white dust food colour. Blend each glaze again until the colour is fully incorporated.

5 Pour each glaze through a fine sieve. Transfer each one to an airtight container and leave in the refrigerator to set overnight.

ALMOND SPONGE

6 Preheat the oven to 200°C (400°F/ gas mark 6). Line a baking tray with silicone paper, sticking it to the tray with cooking oil.

7 Beat together the ground almonds, flour, butter, one whole egg, two egg yolks and 60g (2oz) of caster sugar in a bowl.

8 Whisk the two remaining egg whites and 10g (¼oz) of caster sugar in a stand mixer until it reaches stiff peaks.

RASPBERRY, LEMON AND WHITE CHOCOLATE RING

128

9   Fold one third of the egg whites into the almond mixture until fully combined, then gently fold in the remaining egg whites until fully incorporated.

10   Pour the mixture onto the prepared baking tray and use a large palette knife to gently spread it into a smooth, even layer measuring approximately 26cm x 24cm (10" x 9½"). Bake for eight to 10 minutes until golden brown. Place a piece of baking parchment on top of a wire cooling rack.

11   Leave to cool on the tray for three minutes. Turn the sponge over onto the wire rack covered with baking parchment, take away the tray and gently peel the baking parchment off the back of the sponge. Lay the removed parchment loosely back on top of the sponge to prevent it from drying out. Set aside to cool for approximately 20 minutes.

12   Cut out a 15cm (6") disc of the sponge, then cut a 9cm (3½") disc from its centre.

13   Line the bottom of a 15cm (6") sandwich tin with silicone paper. Place the 15cm (6") sponge ring in the tin then place the 9cm (3½") pâtisserie ring in the centre.

RASPBERRY CREAM

14   Soak the gelatine for five to 10 minutes in enough cold water to cover it.

15   Heat the raspberry pureé to just boiling in a saucepan. Meanwhile, whisk the egg yolks and sugar together in a bowl.

16   Pour the pureé into the egg mixture and whisk until combined. Return the mixture to the saucepan to thicken over a low heat for approximately one minute.

17   Remove from the heat, squeeze the excess water from the gelatine and whisk it in until dissolved. Add the butter and whisk until fully incorporated.

18   Pour the raspberry cream into the cake tin on top of the hazelnut sponge. Place in the freezer for 30 minutes to set.

RASPBERRY JELLY

19   Soak the gelatine for five to 10 minutes in enough cold water to cover it.

20   Bring the raspberry pureé, sugar and cornflour to the boil in a saucepan, stirring with a whisk to prevent lumps from forming. Just as it reaches the boil, remove it from the heat. Squeeze the excess water from the gelatine and add it to the mixture. Stir until dissolved.

21   Pour the jelly on top of the frozen cream in the cake tin (A, B). Leave in the freezer for one to two hours until fully set and frozen.

CHOCOLATE DECORATIONS

22   Place one of the 25cm x 40cm (10" x 16") acetate sheets on the work surface. Pour the white chocolate onto one end of the sheet (C).

23   Place the other acetate sheet on top (D) and use a scraper to scrape the chocolate along the width of the acetate in between the two sheets until it is approximately 1–2mm (¹/₁₆") thick (E). Leave it to set for approximately two minutes.

24   Use 3cm, 4cm and 5cm (1⅛", 1½" and 2") circular cutters to indent into the acetate and cut out the chocolate, twisting the cutter a little as you push it onto the acetate (F). The two acetate sheets should touch and you should be able to see the work surface through the sheets where the circle has been cut.

25   Place the acetate sheets in between two baking trays the keep the chocolate flat and place in the refrigerator for 20 minutes to set. You can leave it in for a little longer if necessary, but not overnight.

WHITE CHOCOLATE AND LEMON MOUSSE

26   Whisk 220ml (7¾fl oz) of the cream to soft-peak consistency and place it in the refrigerator. Place the chocolate in a large mixing bowl.

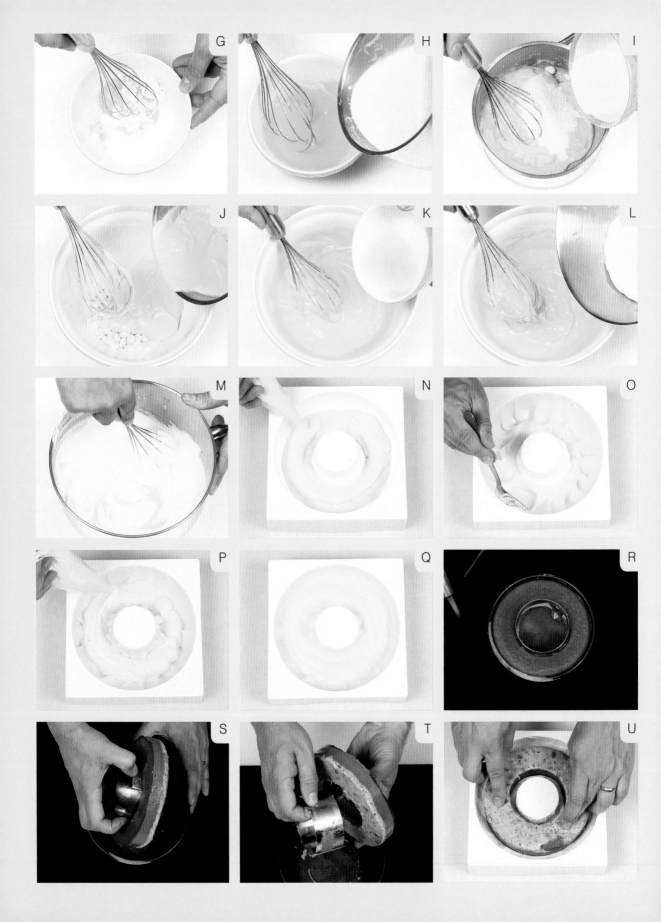

27 Beat the egg yolks, sugar and custard powder together in a bowl (G).

28 Bring the remaining 150ml (5¼fl oz) of cream to the boil in a saucepan. Pour the cream onto the egg mixture (H), stir to combine then return to saucepan and cook for two minutes on a low temperature until thickened.

29 Add the powdered cocoa butter (I) and stir until melted. Pour the mixture into the bowl of white chocolate (J) and whisk until it has all melted. Stir in the lemon zest and juice (K).

30 Fold one third of the whisked whipping cream into the mixture (L). Once combined, fold this mixture into the remaining whisked whipping cream (M). Use straight away.

ASSEMBLY

31 Transfer the mousse to a large piping bag. Snip off the end and pipe some of the mousse into the base of the savarin mould (N).

32 Use the back of a spoon to push the mousse up both sides of the mould to prevent air from getting trapped on the surface (O).

33 Pipe more mousse into the mould (P) until it is 2cm (¾") from the top. Lightly tap the mould on the work surface to level the mousse (Q).

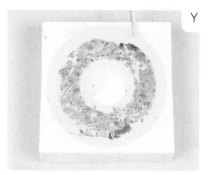

34 Use a blow torch to warm the side of the cake tin containing the fillings to help release them from the tin (R). Lift the fillings out of the cake tin by holding the central pâtisserie ring and sliding everything out together (S). Peel the baking parchment from the base of the sponge if necessary, and remove the pâtisserie ring (T).

35 Place the fillings upside down into the savarin mould, with the sponge layer uppermost and level with the rim of the mould (U). As you push the fillings down some of the mousse may spill out, so fill any remaining gaps around the inner and outer edges with more mousse (V, W).

36 Gently push down on the sponge again to bring it level with the rim of the mould (X). Use a palette knife to scrape off any excess mousse so the contents are all level with the rim of the mould (Y). Place in the freezer to set for approximately three hours.

37 Heat the two glazes to 35–40°C (95–105°F). Pour the white glaze into the pink (Z) and stir a little to create a marbled effect (AA, see overleaf). Place the blade of a palette knife in a jug of hot, boiled water.

AA

AB

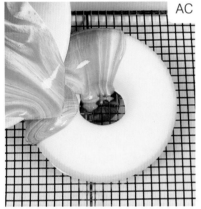

AC

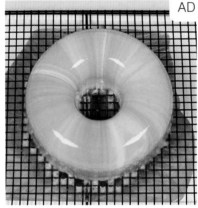

AD

AE

38 Remove the cake from the mould (AB) and place it on a wire rack with a sided baking tray underneath. Pour the mixed glaze all over the cake, making sure the edges are covered too (AC, AD).

39 Leave the cake on the wire rack until it stops dripping, then hold the underside of the entremets with your fingertips and use the wet palette knife to gently wipe the drips onto the underside of the entremets.

40 Wet the palette knife again and use it to help place the entremets in the centre of a clean cake board or serving plate. Slide the palette knife out; the water should help it come away easily.

41 If the entremets is not immediately required it can now be frozen in an airtight container for up to one month: ensure you don't cover over the glaze with cling film or foil as this will spoil the finish. Alternatively, it can be kept in the fridge to fully defrost for approximately four hours, or up to two days, before serving.

42 When ready to serve, remove the chocolate decorations from the refrigerator and peel off the top sheet of acetate. Carefully remove the chocolate discs and gently push them into the top of the cake on one side with some tweezers. Dip the bases of five raspberries in silver dust food colour (AE) and place them between the chocolate discs. Segment the lemon, lay the segments on a baking tray and use a blow torch to burn both sides. Add them between the other decorations.

TRIPLE CHOCOLATE
BERRY TART

This recipe, which includes three different types of chocolate, is sure to become a staple dinner-party dessert. I like to use Ambre Java 36% milk chocolate in the pastry cream as it has a creamy consistency and a balanced flavour of milk and cocoa with a fruity, hazelnut taste to complement the berries.

INGREDIENTS

Chocolate Pastry Cream

250g (8¾oz) milk chocolate, chopped or in callets

3 large egg yolks

100g (3½oz) caster sugar

15g (½oz) cornflour

285ml (10fl oz) semi-skimmed milk

Cocoa Nib Pastry

280g (9¾oz) plain flour, plus extra for dusting and blind-baking

30g (1oz) ground hazelnuts

150g (5¼oz) unsalted butter, cold and cubed, plus extra for greasing

90g (3oz) icing sugar

30g (1oz) cocoa nibs

1 large egg

1 large egg yolk, beaten

Decoration

100g (3½oz) dark chocolate, tempered

300g (10½oz) mixed fresh berries (e.g. raspberries, strawberries, blueberries and blackberries)

Icing sugar, to dust (optional)

EQUIPMENT

Basic equipment (see page 18)

23cm (9") round, 2cm (¾") deep, fluted loose-based flan/tart tin

SERVES 8–10

CHOCOLATE PASTRY CREAM

1 Place the chocolate in a plastic mixing bowl. Whisk together the egg yolks, sugar and cornflour in a separate plastic mixing bowl.

> ### TOP TIP
>
> It's best to use a plastic mixing bowl so the mixture cools quickly after you combine the hot milk with the egg mixture.

2 Heat the milk in a saucepan until it just reaches boiling point. Gradually pour the milk onto the egg mixture (A), whisking continuously until fully combined.

3 Return the mixture to the saucepan and cook on a low heat for three to five minutes, whisking continuously, until thickened.

4 Remove from the heat and pour onto the chocolate (B). Whisk (C) until melted and combined. Cover with cling film touching the surface and leave to cool at room temperature for approximately 20 minutes, then place in the refrigerator until cold.

COCOA NIB PASTRY

5 Beat the flour, ground hazelnuts, butter and icing sugar in a stand mixer fitted with the beater attachment until the mixture has the texture of a crumble (D). Add the cocoa nibs (E).

6 Add a whole egg (F) and continue to beat until the mixture comes together to form a paste (G).

7 Gather the pastry into a ball (H) and place it between two sheets of baking parchment or silicone paper (I). Roll out a circle approximately 25.5cm (10") in diameter and 3–4mm (1⅛–1½") thick (J).

8 Place the rolled-out pastry on a baking tray in the refrigerator to rest for 20 minutes. Meanwhile, butter and flour the 23cm (9") tart tin.

9 Remove the pastry from the fridge and leave to one side for three minutes or until it becomes more pliable before placing it in the tart tin.

10 Lay the rolled-out pastry over the tart tin (K) and ease it down into the tin, gently pushing the pastry into the bottom edge all the way around (L).

TOP TIP

You need approximately 12 fans for the tart, but it's a good idea to make more as spares and to decorate other recipes. The slab will warm up so you will only get time to make about 20 fans at a time. When this happens, place the slab back in the freezer for about 20 minutes. Once it is cold, you can continue to make more fans. Store the fans at room temperature in an airtight container.

11 Fold the pastry over the top edge of the tin and cut away the excess approximately halfway down the outside of the tin with a sharp knife (M). Press the pastry on the outside of the tin into the fluted ridges to hold it in place (N).

12 Place the pastry case in the refrigerator for 10 minutes to rest. Meanwhile, preheat the oven to 170°C (340°F/ gas mark 4).

13 Cut a piece of silicone paper into a circle that is larger than the 23cm (9") tart tin. Scrunch it up to make it more flexible, flatten it out a bit and place it in the centre of the tart tin, pushing the paper down into the bottom edge so that the paper follows the shape of the pastry (O).

14 Fill the silicone paper with flour (P) and blind-bake the pastry case in the preheated oven for 10 minutes until golden brown around the edges.

TOP TIP

I always use flour to blind bake; I find it holds the pastry to the sides of the tin better than baking beans, which in turn stops the pastry from sliding down into the tin. You can keep the flour and use it next time you blind bake.

15 Lift the silicone paper filled with flour out of the tart tin. Use a fork to prick the base of the tart and return it to the oven for a further 10–15 minutes, or until the base is golden brown.

16 Immediately brush the cooked pastry with beaten egg yolk and leave it to cool in the tin on a wire rack (if you're worried about the egg cooking, return it to the oven for two minutes before cooling). Once completely cool, trim the edges with a small palette knife.

TOP TIP

As an alternative to egg yolk, you could sieve a fine layer of powdered cocoa butter over the pastry.

CHOCOLATE FANS

17 Place the marble slab in the freezer for a minimum of three hours (overnight if possible). Line a baking tray with a sheet of silicone paper or acetate.

18 Use the end of a cranked palette knife to pick up a small amount of melted, tempered chocolate. Spread the chocolate onto the frozen slab: aim to make a rough rectangle shape (Q).

19 Very quickly use the edge of the palette knife to cut down the middle of the chocolate rectangle lengthways (R) and to cut off the two ends. You should end up with two long rectangular strips, each with a rough edge along one of the longest sides.

20 Using just the fingertips of both of your hands, pick up one of the strips. Hold it with the rough edge towards you and the cut edge facing away from you. Concertina the rough edge (S) and pinch the ends together to create a fan shape (T). Repeat with the second strip. Set the two fans aside on the prepared baking tray. Scrape any excess chocolate from the marble slab then wipe it clean with some kitchen paper and start again.

ASSEMBLY

21 Remove the chocolate pastry cream from the refrigerator and re-whisk it, ensuring there are no lumps. Pour the pastry cream into the cooled, baked pastry case (U) and level it with a small, cranked palette knife (V).

22 Remove the pastry case from the tin and place it onto a presentation plate. If you're worried the tart will slide off, secure it with a little pastry cream in the centre of the plate. Arrange the berries on top of the filling (W) and add the chocolate fans in between. Finish with a dusting of icing sugar if desired.

WHITE CHOCOLATE & LEMON MERINGUE

CHEESECAKE

This recipe brings together two of my favourite desserts: lemon meringue pie and
zesty cheesecake. White chocolate makes the cheesecake extra creamy while the
chocolate flower adds a professional finishing touch.

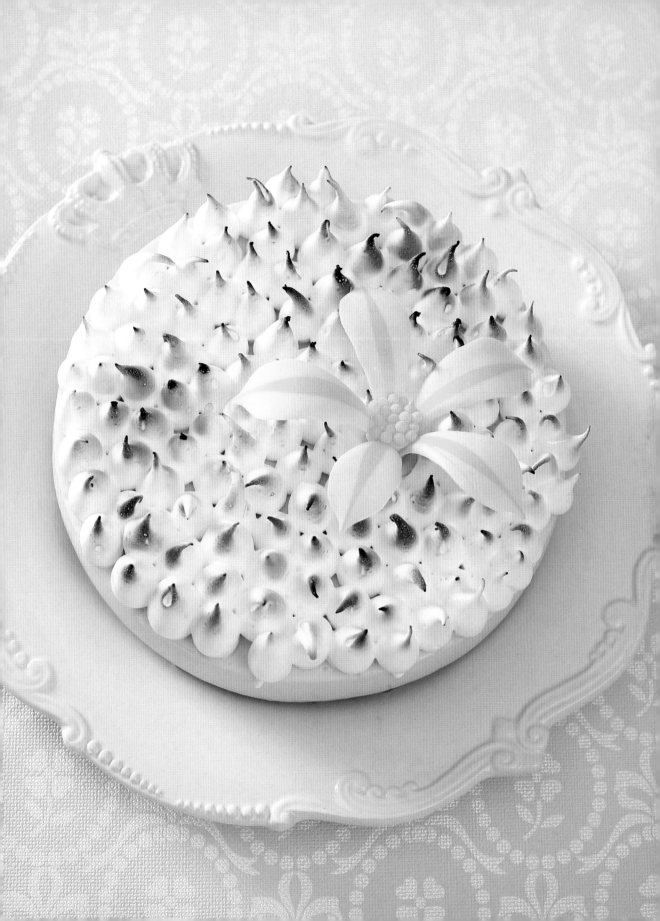

INGREDIENTS

Biscuit Base

200g (7oz) chocolate biscuits, e.g. chocolate digestives

40g (1½oz) unsalted butter

Lemon Cheesecake

3 sheets of leaf gelatine

250g (8¾oz) white chocolate

250ml (8¾fl oz) whipping cream

50g (1¾oz) egg yolks (approximately 3 large egg yolks)

75g (2½oz) caster sugar

20ml (¾fl oz) lemon juice

250g (8¾oz) full-fat cream cheese

2 lemons, zest only

Chocolate Flower

15 x 4mm (³/₁₆") diameter white pearlescent ball dragées (SK)

1tsp Yellow dust food colour (SK)

200g (7oz) white chocolate, tempered

Meringue Topping

150g (5¼oz) caster sugar

65g (2¼oz) egg whites (approximately 2 medium egg whites)

EQUIPMENT

Basic equipment (see page 18)

18cm (7") diameter, 4cm (1½") deep pâtisserie ring

15cm x 10cm (6" x 4") acetate

6–7cm (2³/₈–2¾") circular cutter

1cm (³/₈") plain round piping nozzle

Chef's blow torch

SERVES 8–10

BISCUIT BASE

1   Place a sheet of kitchen foil on the work surface and lay a sheet of silicone paper on top. Place the pâtisserie ring in the centre of the paper and scrunch the kitchen foil around the base of the ring to hold it in place (A). Place on a baking tray lined with a non-stick mat (this prevents the ring from sliding around on the tray).

2   Blitz the biscuits to small crumbs in a food processor.

3   Melt the butter and pour it into the food processor, blitzing it for a few seconds to mix.

4   Spoon the biscuit mixture into the bottom of the ring and push it down with a small cranked palette knife (B).

LEMON CHEESECAKE

5   Place the gelatine in a small bowl with enough cold water to cover it for five minutes to soften.

6   Melt the chocolate in a microwave or bain-marie. Semi-whip the cream.

7   Remove the gelatine from the water and transfer it to a bowl. Add a little of the semi-whipped cream. Melt the gelatine into the cream over a bain-marie or in the microwave for 10 seconds. Stir to ensure it is fully melted.

8   Place the egg yolks, sugar and lemon juice together in the bowl of a stand mixer and whisk to combine, then heat them gently over a bain-marie until they are warm and the sugar has dissolved. Remove from the heat.

9   Fit the bowl of egg and sugar mixture to a stand mixer fitted with the whisk attachment. Whisk for approximately one minute then add the gelatine and cream mixture and continue whisking for two more minutes (C).

10   While it's still warm, add the melted white chocolate to the mixture (D) and continue whisking until fully incorporated.

11   In a mixing bowl, beat the cream cheese a little to remove any lumps then add the remaining whipped cream (E). Fold the white chocolate mixture into the cream cheese (F).

12   Add the lemon zest to the mixture (G) and fold it in until evenly distributed.

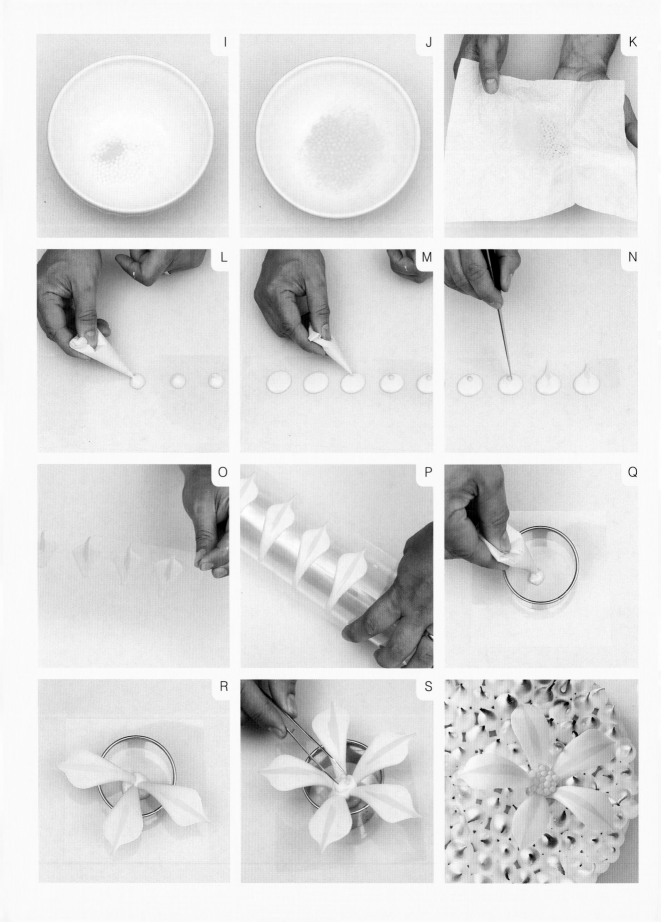

13 Pour the cheesecake mixture over the biscuit base (H, see page 143). Give it a gentle shake or tap it on the worktop to ensure it is level and has no air bubbles. Place the cheesecake in the freezer for two hours or until fully set and frozen. The cheesecake can be frozen without the topping for up to two months.

TOP TIP

It's best to freeze the cheesecake at this stage rather than leaving it to set in the refrigerator; this will make it easier to remove the pâtisserie ring.

CHOCOLATE FLOWER

14 Pour the white pearlescent ball dragées into a small bowl and add ½tsp of yellow dust food colour (I). Give the bowl a gentle shake to coat the pearls with the dust (J). Pour the sugar pearls into a sheet of kitchen paper and shake again (K).

15 Colour 50g (1¾oz) of the tempered white chocolate yellow with ½tsp of yellow dust food colour and place it in a small piping bag. Place the remaining tempered white chocolate in another piping bag.

16 Place the acetate sheet horizontally on a flat work surface. Pipe six 1cm (³⁄₈") diameter dots along the top of the sheet, leaving a 2–4cm (¾–1½") gap between each one (L).

17 Immediately pipe a dot of yellow-coloured chocolate at the base of each white dot (M).

18 Pull a knife or cocktail stick through the two chocolate dots to make a point at the base (N).

19 Lift up the acetate sheet, holding the dots at the top, and let the chocolate drip down to create petal shapes (O). The chocolate will all set at slightly different rates; you can trim the petals at a later stage if necessary.

20 Lay the acetate strip over a cylindrical object, securing with a dot of chocolate underneath each corner (P), and set them aside until touch-dry. Transfer the petals to the refrigerator to fully set; this should take approximately 20 minutes.

21 Once set, carefully remove the petals from the strip of acetate. You may need to trim some of the ends with a warm, sharp knife so they are all the same size.

22 Place the circular cutter on a square of acetate and pipe a little tempered white chocolate in the centre (Q). Arrange five petals around the edge of the cutter so the tips meet in the chocolate centre (R).

23 Pipe a little more chocolate over the join between the petals and place the yellow ball dragées on top with tweezers (S). Leave the flower to set at room temperature.

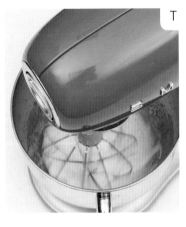

MERINGUE TOPPING

24 Pour 140g (5oz) of the caster sugar and 40ml (1½fl oz) of water into a saucepan and place it over a medium heat.

25 Meanwhile, place the egg whites in the bowl of a stand mixer with the remaining 10g (¼oz) of caster sugar. Whisk the mixture (T) until it forms stiff peaks.

26 When the sugar syrup reaches 118°C (244°F), switch the stand mixer to a low speed and pour the syrup into the egg whites (U). Once all the sugar syrup is added, turn up the mixer to a medium speed and keep whisking until cool: this could take 10–15 minutes.

ASSEMBLY

27 Release the cheesecake by heating the ring with a blow torch or a warm cloth and place it on a serving plate (V).

28 Transfer the meringue mixture to a large piping bag fitted with a 1cm (³/₈") round nozzle. Starting in the centre and working outwards, pipe peaks on top of the cheesecake until the whole surface is covered (W).

29 Use a blow torch to scorch the tops of the meringue peaks (X). Place the chocolate flower on top of the cheesecake (Y).

30 Store the cheesecake in the refrigerator for up to two days.

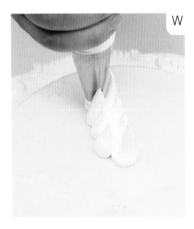

SHOWSTOPPERS

CHOCOLATE
SPLATTER
CROQUEMBOUCHE

This colourful take on a traditional croquembouche would be a vibrant centrepiece for any special occasion. You can't really go wrong with the chocolate splatters and it's a lot of fun – just channel your inner Jackson Pollock!

INGREDIENTS

Sablé Biscuit Topping

170g (5¾oz) unsalted butter

200g (7oz) granulated sugar

200g (7oz) plain flour

Dust food colours: Daffodil, Orange, Poinsettia and Vine (SK)

Choux Pastry

120ml (4¼fl oz) semi-skimmed milk

100g (3½oz) salted butter, cubed

Pinch of salt

Pinch of sugar

140g (5oz) plain flour, sifted

4–6 medium eggs, beaten

Chocolate Discs

1kg (2lb 3¼oz) white chocolate, tempered

50g (1¾oz) powdered cocoa butter, melted to 32°C (90°F)

Dust food colours: Daffodil, Orange, Poinsettia and Vine (SK)

White Chocolate and Raspberry Mousse

375g (13¼oz) raspberry purée

35g (1¼oz) custard powder

35g (1¼oz) caster sugar

85g (2¾oz) egg yolks (approximately 5 medium egg yolks)

75g (2½oz) powdered cocoa butter (SK)

190g (6¾oz) white chocolate, chopped or in callets

550ml (1pt) whipping cream

Buttercream

400g (14oz) unsalted butter, cubed and softened

400g (14oz) icing sugar

1tsp vanilla paste

EQUIPMENT

Basic equipment (see page 18)

Half-sphere silicone moulds: 4 x 3cm (1⅛") (Silikomart)

Circular cutters: 3cm and 4cm (1⅛" and 1½")

Acetate sheets: 2 x 25cm x 40cm (10" x 16")

Croquembouche cone: 50cm tall x 15cm wide (20" x 6")

5mm (¼") plain round piping nozzle

MAKES ONE CROQUEMBOUCHE TOWER, APPROXIMATELY 96 BUNS

SABLÉ BISCUIT TOPPING

1 Cream together the butter and sugar in a stand mixer fitted with the paddle attachment (A). Scrape the sides of the bowl, add the flour and mix until fully combined (B).

2 Bring the dough together using your hands (C), then divide the dough between four bowls. Colour the pieces red, orange, green and yellow respectively by kneading 1–2 level tsp of dust food colour into the dough (D–G).

TOP TIP

Wear food-grade plastic gloves when kneading the dough to prevent the food colour from staining your hands.

3 Roll out each colour of dough between two sheets of silicone paper to a thickness of approximately 3mm (⅛") (H, I). Place in the refrigerator to rest while you make the choux pastry.

CHOUX PASTRY

4 Heat the milk, butter, salt, sugar and 130ml (4½fl oz) of water together in a saucepan (J) until boiling.

5 Remove from the heat, add all of the sifted flour at once and stir to combine (K, L).

6 Place the pan back over a medium heat, stirring to help dry out the mixture (M, see page 154). Remove from the heat when the

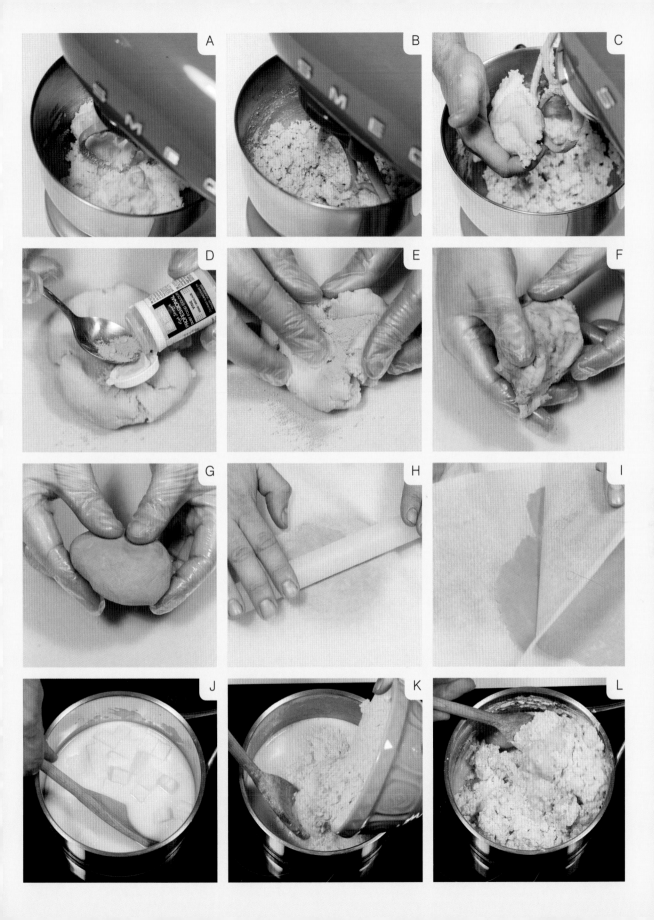

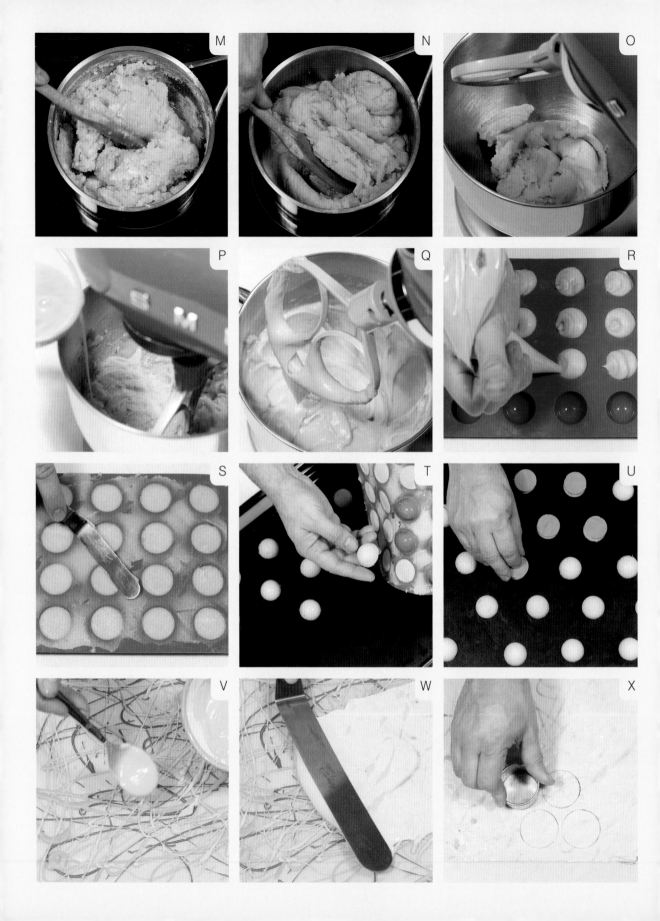

pastry starts to break into small pieces and is a little crumbly in texture with a slight shine to it (N) – this should take three or four minutes.

7   Transfer the mixture a stand mixer fitted with the paddle attachment (O). Beat the mixture at a slow speed for a couple of minutes to cool it slightly then gradually add the eggs a little at a time (P) until it becomes a glossy, soft paste that falls off a spoon or the beater with a molten, gradual drop (Q). You may not need to add all of the eggs to reach this consistency.

8   Transfer the mixture to a large piping bag and pipe it into the 3cm (1¹/₈") half-sphere moulds (R). Scrape off any excess mixture using a palette knife to flatten the tops (S). Place in the freezer to set for one to two hours or until the half-spheres pop out of the mould easily.

TOP TIP

If you don't own half-sphere moulds, pipe 3cm (1¹/₈") buns on a baking tray lined with silicone paper instead.

9   Preheat the oven to 175°C (345°F/gas mark 5) and line two baking trays with silicone mats. Pop the frozen half-spheres out of the first mould and spread them out evenly over one of the trays, leaving at least 3cm (1¹/₈") between them (T). Repeat with the second half-sphere mould so you have two trays of buns ready for the oven.

10   Cut out 24 3cm (1¹/₈") circles from one colour of the sablé biscuit dough and place them on top of each choux bun on one of the trays, pressing down gently (U). Repeat using a different colour for the second batch of buns. Leave the pastry to defrost slightly for 10 minutes at room temperature.

11   Place both trays in the oven and bake for 15 minutes, then reduce the heat to 160°C (325°F/gas mark 3) and bake for a further 15 minutes.

TOP TIP

If you see that the tops of the buns are colouring a bit too much, quickly place a piece of silicone paper on top of them without opening the oven door for too long.

12   Once the buns have finished cooking, turn off the oven, prop the oven door open slightly with a wooden spoon and leave to cool down for 10–15 minutes. Remove the buns from the oven and, when they're completely cool, use a 5mm (¼") plain round piping nozzle to make a hole in the bottom of each one.

13   Repeat steps 9–12 to bake the buns from the remaining two half-sphere moulds.

CHOCOLATE DISCS

14   Divide 400g (14oz) of tempered white chocolate evenly between four small bowls. Add 1tbsp of melted cocoa butter and ½tsp of green, red, yellow or orange dust food colour to each bowl and mix thoroughly.

15   Place two acetate sheets on the work surface and use a spoon to drizzle each colour of chocolate over the sheets in turn (V). Leave until touch-dry.

16   Pour approximately 200g (7oz) of tempered white chocolate in the middle of each sheet. Use a palette knife to spread out the chocolate thinly (W) so it completely covers the acetate sheet. Leave until touch-dry.

17   Use a 4cm (1½") round cutter to cut the chocolate into discs, but do not pull them off the acetate sheet at this stage (X). When you have done this for both sheets, cover them with another acetate sheet or silicone paper and place them between two baking trays to keep them flat. Place them in the refrigerator to set for 30 minutes.

18   Use a pastry brush to cover the croquembouche cone with any leftover tempered white chocolate then leave it to set.

WHITE CHOCOLATE AND RASPBERRY MOUSSE

19 Bring the raspberry purée to the boil in a saucepan. Meanwhile, whisk the custard powder, sugar and egg yolks together in a small bowl (Y). Place the chocolate in a mixing bowl.

20 Stir a little of the hot purée into the egg mixture (Z), then pour it all back into the saucepan and cook over a low heat until thickened (AA, AB).

21 Remove from the heat and add the powdered cocoa butter (AC). Mix until fully incorporated (AD) then pour the mixture over the chocolate (AE). Stir until the chocolate has melted (AF).

22 Semi-whip the cream and fold it into the raspberry mixture (AG, AH). Refrigerate for one hour.

23 Once cool, transfer the mousse to a large piping bag fitted with a 5mm (¼") plain round nozzle. Pipe it into the centre of the choux buns.

BUTTERCREAM

24 Beat the butter, icing sugar and vanilla paste together in a stand mixer until light and fluffy.

25 Fit a large piping bag with a 5mm (¼") round nozzle and fill it with the buttercream.

ASSEMBLY

26 Remove the chocolate discs by peeling back the acetate backing sheet (AI). Use a little buttercream to stick one disc centrally to the front of each bun.

27 Sort the buns into groups of each colour. Pipe a little buttercream onto the back of each bun and stick them around the bottom of the cone. Work around the cone in layers, starting at the bottom and arranging the colours evenly (AJ).

CHOCOLATE LOVERS'
WEDDING CAKE

Fruit cakes, marzipan and royal icing have fallen out of favour in recent years so
I've brought the traditional trio up to date with these delicious, chocolaty versions.
The best thing about this cake is that you can make it up to three months in
advance, leaving you plenty of time to relax in the run-up to the big day.

INGREDIENTS

Chocolate Fruit Cakes

Square cake size	10cm (4")	15cm (6")	20.5cm (8")
Currants	150g (5¼oz)	350g (12¼oz)	700g (1lb 8¾oz)
Sultanas	75g (2½oz)	150g (5¼oz)	300g (10½oz)
Raisins	75g (2½oz)	150g (5¼oz)	300g (10½oz)
Dried cherries	35g (1¼oz)	70g (2½oz)	140g (5oz)
Orange, zest and juice	½	1	1½
Chocolate liqueur (or liqueur of your choice)	50ml (1¾fl oz)	100ml (3½fl oz)	150ml (5¼fl oz)
Unsalted butter, at room temperature	85g (2¾oz)	170g (5¾oz)	340g (12oz)
Soft, dark brown sugar	85g (2¾oz)	170g (5¾oz)	340g (12oz)
Large eggs, at room temperature, beaten	2	3	4
Black treacle (molasses)	1tbsp	2tbsp	3tbsp
Plain flour	85g (2¾oz)	175g (6oz)	350g (12¼oz)
Cocoa powder	20g (¾oz)	40g (1½oz)	80g (2¾oz)
Ground cinnamon	½tsp	1tsp	1½tsp
Ground ginger	½tsp	1tsp	1½tsp
Dark chocolate baking chips	50g (1¾oz)	100g (3½oz)	150g (5¼oz)
Ground hazelnuts	25g (>¾oz)	50g (1¾oz)	100g (3½oz)
Silicone paper strip	12cm x 45cm (4½inch x 18inch)	12cm x 65cm (4½inch x 25½inch)	12cm x 85cm (4½ inch x 33.46 inch)
Baking time	45–60 minutes	1½–2 hours	2–2½ hours
Servings (2.5cm/1" square portions)	16	36	64

MAKES 110 COFFEE PORTIONS

Chocolate Marzipan

2kg (4lb 6½oz) marzipan

70g (2½oz) cocoa powder

Chocolate Royal Icing

1kg (2lb 3¼oz) icing sugar

30g (1oz) dried albumen

25g (¾oz) concentrated brown paste food colour (ProGel®)

½tsp chocolate flavouring (optional)

3tsp glycerine

Assembly

200g (7oz) apricot glaze (boiled, sieved apricot jam)

Decorations

250g (8¾oz) milk chocolate modelling paste (SK)

Gold edible metallic paint (SK)

EQUIPMENT

Basic equipment (see page 18)

Square cake tins, 7.5cm (3") deep: 10cm, 15cm and 20.5cm (4", 6" and 8")

Cake drums: 10cm, 15cm, 20.5cm and 25.5cm (4", 6", 8" and 10")

Marzipan spacers

2 cake smoothers

Cake cards: 15cm, 20.5cm and 25.5cm (6", 8" and 10")

Icing ruler

Side scraper

9 cake dowels

Silicone moulds: Acanthus Leaf Garland and Small Acanthus Leaves (SK)

Paintbrush: no. 10

3.1m (3yd 14") x 1.5cm (½") width double-faced gold satin ribbon

Double-sided tape

CHOCOLATE FRUIT CAKES

1 Stir together the dried fruit, orange zest, orange juice and chocolate liqueur in a bowl. Cover the bowl with cling film and leave to stand for 24 hours, stirring the mixture occasionally.

2 Prepare the cake tins: cut a strip of silicone paper to the size specified in the table opposite. Make a 2.5cm (1") fold along one long side of the strip. Use a pair of scissors to make regular cuts along the fold (A). Use the base of the cake tin as a guide to cut out a square of paper (B). Brush the inside of the tin with oil or melted butter (C). Place the long strip around the inside of the tin, pushing the folded section onto the base (D). Place the square paper in the base of the tin (E). Use a knife to carefully help push the paper into the corners of the tin for a sharp finish (F).

3 To protect the outside of the cake, wrap a strip of brown paper around the tin so it overlaps slightly and secure it with string. Preheat the oven to 140°C (275°F/gas mark 1).

4 Cream the butter and brown sugar together until light and fluffy (G). Scrape down the sides of the bowl then add the eggs a little at a time (H), continuing to mix until they are all incorporated.

5 Fold in the black treacle, then sift in the flour, cocoa powder, cinnamon and ground ginger (I). Mix until fully incorporated (J). If you feel the mixture

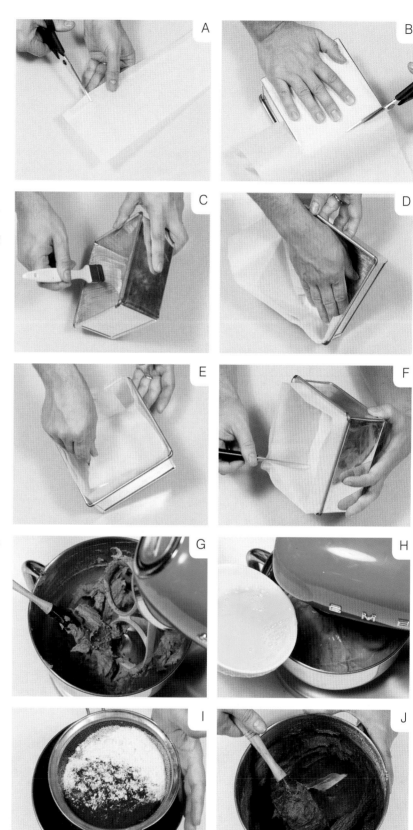

is a little dry, stir in a small amount of milk. It is the correct consistency when the mixture falls off a spoon within a few seconds.

6   Stir in the dried fruit, orange zest, orange juice and chocolate liqueur (K), followed by the dark chocolate baking chips and ground hazelnuts (L).

7   Spoon the mixture into the lined cake tins, level it (M) then sprinkle a little water on top of each one. Cut a square of baking parchment to the size of the tin and place it flat on top of each cake (N).

TOP TIP

If you have a cake board or the base of a loose-bottomed cake tin the same size as the tin you are using, place it on top of the paper to keep in the moisture and prevent a dry crust from forming.

8   Bake in the oven for the recommended time or until a cake tester inserted in the centre of the cake comes out clean.

9   Leave to cool in the tins for an hour, then remove the cakes and place them on a wire rack to cool completely. Once cool, wrap the cakes in a layer of greaseproof paper followed by aluminium foil.

CHOCOLATE MARZIPAN

10   Warm the marzipan gently in the microwave or leave it in a warm place until slightly soft. This will make it easier to knead.

11   Knead the cocoa power into the marzipan until it is fully incorporated (O, P). Wrap the paste in cling film until it is needed.

COVERING THE CAKES WITH MARZIPAN

12   Cover the cakes in marzipan one at a time. First, use a serrated knife to level the top of the fruit cake. Fill in any holes in the fruit cake with pieces of marzipan; this will help achieve a smooth coating. Attach the cake to a drum of the same size using a little royal icing.

13   Brush the top of the cake with warm, boiled apricot glaze (Q). Roll out some marzipan on a work surface dusted with icing sugar to a thickness of 6mm (¼") using marzipan spacers (R). Cut it to the size of the top of the cake, using a ruler and sharp knife to ensure it is a perfect square (S). Place the marzipan square on top of the cake (T).

TOP TIP

Always use icing sugar to prevent sticking rather than cornflour when rolling out marzipan; cornflour can cause bacteria to grow on the cake surface.

14   Brush the sides of the cake with warm glaze. Roll out some marzipan into a strip that is slightly longer than the width of the cake and slightly wider than the height, including the cake drum, allowing for 5–7mm (¼– ⅜") extra at each end of the strip. Cut a straight line along the bottom edge. Repeat to make three more lengths of marzipan in the same way.

15   Place a strip of marzipan along one side of the cake at a time, ensuring the straight edge is flush with the bottom of the cake drum. Use a sharp knife to trim away the excess marzipan from the sides and from the top of the cake, using the top layer of marzipan as a guide. Attach the next length of marzipan to the opposite side.

16   Repeat this around the remaining sides of the cake then use two cake smoothers to smooth over the top and sides. Use a knife to neaten the joins along the top and down the sides of the cake if necessary. Allow the marzipan to dry overnight (U) – place kitchen paper loosely on top to protect it from dust. In the meantime, make the royal icing as this also needs to rest overnight.

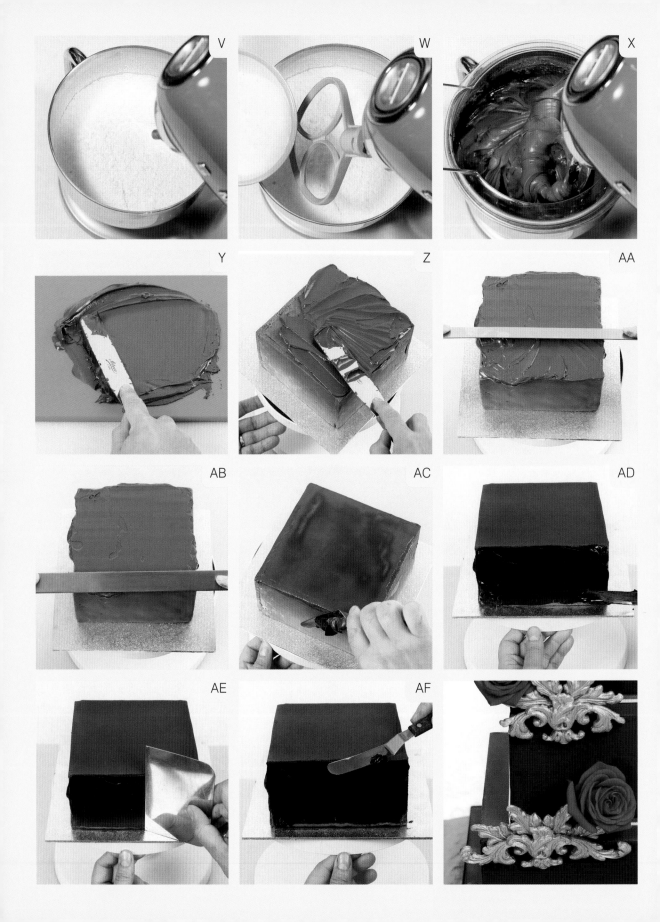

CHOCOLATE ROYAL ICING

17   Sift the icing sugar into the bowl of a stand mixer fitted with the paddle attachment (V).

18   Pour 170ml (5¾fl oz) of water into a small bowl and gradually hand-whisk the albumen into it. Pour it over the icing sugar (W).

19   Cover the top of the machine with a tea towel to prevent the icing sugar from escaping, then slowly start the mixer. Keep it covered until the mixture becomes a paste then remove the cloth and mix the icing on a slow speed for eight minutes or until the mixture reaches stiff-peak consistency.

20   Mix in the brown paste food colour and chocolate flavouring until they are fully incorporated (X). Don't mix in the glycerine at this stage. Cover with cling film touching the surface of the icing and leave to rest overnight.

COVERING THE CAKES WITH ROYAL ICING

21   Reserve 40g (1½oz) of royal icing in an airtight container to coat the board later. Add the glycerine to the remaining royal icing and stir well. Without glycerine the icing will become too hard to cut.

22   Place the first cake on cake card 5cm (2") larger than the cake, and then onto a turntable. Use a palette knife to put one to two tablespoons of royal icing onto a clean and grease-free board and paddle the icing: keeping the knife in contact with the icing, spread the icing backwards and forwards until it looks smooth and shiny (Y). This action removes large air bubbles and makes the icing more fluid.

23   Use the palette knife to transfer the icing to the centre of the cake. Spread the icing across the top by paddling it again: keep the end of the palette knife in the centre of the cake and use small paddling motions (Z). Move the turntable at the same time until the icing is spread evenly across the top of the cake to the edge.

24   Wipe an icing ruler with a clean, damp cloth and rest one long side gently on the far edge of the cake at an acute angle (i.e. tipped towards you). Using even pressure, pull the ruler towards you (AA). Swivel the top of the ruler on the front edge of the cake and push away from you (AB); if the icing doesn't have a smooth finish then pull the ruler back towards you across the cake once more, continuing off the cake to finish.

25   Use a clean palette knife to trim away any excess icing from the edge by cutting straight down away from the wet icing (AC). Put the cake aside to dry under a balanced-arm lamp for two to three hours and clean all tools. (You don't have to use the lamp; the drying process will just take longer.)

26   Place the cake back on the turntable to cover the sides. Paddle some royal icing and spread it over one side of the cake. Hold the palette knife in a vertical position against the cake and paddle the icing to spread and smooth it over the side of the cake (AD).

27   Wipe the side scraper with a clean, damp cloth. Hold the scraper at one end of the royal-iced side at an acute angle. In one smooth movement, draw the scraper across the side (AE) and off the cake, keeping the lower side of the scraper against the cake drum. Trim away the excess icing from the top and sides by cutting away from the wet icing with a palette knife (AF). Clean up the icing from the cake drum. Repeat on the opposite side then set aside to dry under a balanced-arm lamp for two to three hours.

28   When dry, repeat to royal ice the two remaining sides of the cake. Set aside to dry, then remove any lumps gently with a sharp knife.

29   Repeat steps 22–28 to do the first coat of royal icing on the remaining two cakes. Repeat the steps twice more on each cake to give all of the cakes three coats in total. Once the third coat is dry, carefully remove the cakes with their drums from the cake cards.

30   To coat the cake drum, add cooled, boiled water drop by drop into the reserved glycerine-free icing to make it thinner. It is the correct consistency when a clean knife

drawn across the icing leaves a line which disappears on the count of 16–18 seconds. If it takes longer then add more water; if it's quicker then stir in a little more sifted icing sugar. Cover with a clean, damp cloth and leave to stand for 30 minutes.

31　Disperse any surface bubbles by gently stirring the icing. Using a palette knife, thickly spread the icing onto the drum and use the same method for covering the top of the cake to cover the cake drum. Clean the edges and leave to dry completely before stacking the cakes.

STACKING THE CAKES

32　Spread a little royal icing in the centre of the iced cake drum and place the 20.5cm (8") cake on top, ensuring it is central.

33　Insert five evenly spaced dowels into the 20.5cm (8") cake and mark the points where they meet the top of the cake. Remove the dowels, trim them at the marked points and reinsert them into their original positions.

34　Spread a little royal icing over the dowelled area and place the 15cm (6") cake on top. Repeat this process, using four dowels in the second tier and placing the 10cm (4") cake on top. Set the cake aside to firm for one hour.

MAKING THE DECORATIONS

35　Make one Acanthus leaf garland and four Acanthus leaves for each tier. Knead a small piece of chocolate modelling paste then press it firmly into the silicone mould (AG, AH). Level the paste at the back with a small palette knife (AI); sharp knives can damage the silicone. Leave

the piece to set for approximately five minutes then flex the mould gently to release the shape (AJ).

36　For the bottom tier leave the decorations whole, for the middle tier use a small palette knife to cut away a section on either side of the garland, and for the top tier cut away a further section so just the central part of the garland remains. You will also need to trim the base of the leaves for the top tier (AK, AL).

37　Place each decoration on a piece of silicone paper. Use a paintbrush and gold edible metallic paint to paint the decorations (AM), ensuring the colour gets into all the details of each piece. Leave to set for 20 minutes at room temperature.

FINISHING TOUCHES

38　Wrap gold ribbon around the edge of each cake board, fixing it in place at the back with double-sided tape.

39　Attach the moulded decorations to the top left corner of each tier with a little royal icing: place the four scrolls in a fan shape first, then attach the garland pieces on top.

40　Store in a cool, dry area in a cake box for up to three months.

TOP TIP

Fresh, food-safe flowers are great for adding an extra dimension to cakes: insert the stalk into a plastic posy pick then insert that into the cake on the day of serving.

DOUBLE-BARREL
CHOCOLATE & PEANUT BUTTER
LAYER CAKE

Double-height cakes look impressive but they can be tricky to construct.
In this recipe, I share the tricks of the trade to help you make it a success.

INGREDIENTS

Chocolate Ganache

1kg (2lb 3¼oz) dark chocolate, chopped or in callets

500ml (17¾fl oz) whipping cream

Chocolate Cake

375g (13¼oz) unsalted butter

300g (10½oz) dark chocolate, chopped or in callets

100ml (3½fl oz) semi-skimmed milk

2tbsp instant coffee

2tsp vanilla paste

375g (13¼oz) soft, dark brown sugar

6 large eggs, beaten

200g (7oz) self-raising flour

200g (7oz) plain flour

1tsp bicarbonate of soda

60g (2oz) cocoa powder

225ml (8fl oz) soured cream

Peanut Butter Ganache

450g (1lb) white chocolate, chopped or in callets

150ml (5¼fl oz) whipping cream

1tsp vanilla paste

150g (5¼oz) smooth peanut butter

Caramelised Peanuts

125g (4½oz) salted peanuts

90g (3oz) sugar

Decoration

150g (5¼oz) white chocolate, tempered

200g (7oz) dark chocolate, tempered

3tsp Purple dust food colour (SK)

Fresh, food-safe flowers

EQUIPMENT

Basic equipment (see page 18)

3 x 15cm (6") round, 7cm (2¾") deep cake tins

2 x 1cm (³⁄₈") plain round piping nozzles

Round cake boards: 1 x 12.5cm and 4 x 15cm (1 x 5" and 4 x 6")

Metal side scraper

5cm x 1m (2" x 39") acetate strip

MAKES 24 DESSERT PORTIONS OR
48 COFFEE PORTIONS

CHOCOLATE GANACHE

1   Melt the chocolate and heat it to 32°C (90°F) in a microwave or bain-marie. Meanwhile, bring the cream to the boil in a saucepan then allow it cool to approximately 38°C (100°F).

2   Once they are both at the correct temperature, pour the cream into the chocolate and use a hand blender to blend them together (A–C). Transfer the ganache to an airtight container and cover with some cling film against the surface of the ganache. Allow to cool to room temperature then leave the ganache to set in the refrigerator overnight.

TOP TIP

I have used this method for the ganache (rather than pouring hot cream over solid chocolate) as having the cream and chocolate at similar temperatures helps to prevent them from splitting when they are mixed. The ganache is going to be visible on the side of the cake so it's important to get a good finish which doesn't bloom.

CHOCOLATE CAKE

3   Preheat the oven to 150°C (300°F/ gas mark 2). Grease and line three 15cm (6") round cake tins.

4   Place the butter, chocolate, milk, coffee and vanilla in a bain-marie and whisk together (D) until melted and fully combined (E).

5   Remove from the heat and transfer to the bowl of a stand mixer

fitted with a paddle attachment. Add the sugar (F, see page 173) then mix in the eggs (G) at a low speed.

6   Sift the flours, cocoa powder and bicarbonate of soda into a bowl. Beat the dry ingredients into the chocolate mixture at a low speed (H) until fully incorporated. Mix in the soured cream.

7   Divide the mixture between the three prepared cake tins and bake for between 1 hour 20 minutes and 1 hour 35 minutes, or until a skewer inserted into the centre comes out clean. Place on a wire rack to cool in the tins for one hour, then remove from the tins and cool fully.

PEANUT BUTTER GANACHE

8   Melt the white chocolate and heat it to 32°C (90°F) in a microwave or bain-marie. Meanwhile, bring the cream and vanilla paste to the boil in a saucepan then allow it cool to approximately 38°C (100°F).

9   Once they are both at the correct temperature, pour the cream into the chocolate (I) and whisk together until fully combined (J).

10   Whisk in the peanut butter (K) then set aside at room temperature to cool and thicken.

CARAMELISED PEANUTS

11   Preheat the oven to 160°C (325°F/gas mark 2).

12   Spread out the peanuts on a baking tray and roast them in the oven for 15–20 minutes, or until darkened slightly. Leave to cool, then roughly chop.

13   Heat the sugar and 25ml (>¾fl oz) of water in a medium saucepan to 119°C (246°F). Add the roasted peanuts while they are still warm, stirring continuously.

14   The sugar and water will take on a sandy texture; keep the pan on a medium heat until the sugar returns to a liquid caramel. Take the saucepan off the heat and pour the caramelised nuts onto the lined baking tray. Set aside to cool at room temperature for 30 minutes.

15   Once cold, break up the nuts if necessary and place them in an airtight container.

ASSEMBLY

16   Trim the tops of the three cakes with a serrated knife to make them level (L), then cut each one in half to make six layers (M). Transfer the peanut butter ganache to a large piping bag fitted with a 1cm (³/₈") plain round nozzle.

17   Place the first layer of cake on a 15cm (6") cake board, securing it with a little ganache. Pipe a spiral of peanut butter ganache from the centre of the cake outwards, stopping approximately 1cm (³/₈") from the edge (N).

18   Warm the chocolate ganache gently in a microwave then blend it with a hand blender until it reaches a spreadable paste consistency.

TOP TIP

When you use the chocolate ganache, reheat it gently to reach a spreadable consistency. Be careful to not overheat the ganache; if it gets too hot, fat bloom will appear on the sides of the cake as the chocolate will no longer be tempered.

19   Place a small amount of ganache in a piping bag fitted with a 1cm (³/₈") plain round nozzle. Pipe a circle around the peanut butter ganache at the edge of the cake.

20   Sprinkle a quarter of the caramelised peanuts over the peanut butter ganache (O). Place the second layer of cake on top (P) and press down gently (Q).

21   Pipe another layer of peanut butter ganache and chocolate ganache on top, and add the caramelised peanuts as before. Place a third layer of cake on top and press down gently.

22   Repeat steps 17–21 with the other three layers of cake on a second 15cm (6") cake board.

23 Attach another 15cm (6") cake board upside down on top of each filled cake with a little chocolate ganache.

24 Cover one cake at a time with chocolate ganache. Pick up the cake, holding it between the cake boards, and use a large palette knife to spread ganache over the sides of the cake (R, S). Remove the excess ganache and create a smooth layer in line with the edges of the cake boards using a metal side scraper. Repeat with the second cake. Place them both in the refrigerator to set for one hour.

25 Warm the blade of a palette knife in hot, boiled water then dry it with some kitchen paper. Use the hot palette knife to remove the 15cm (6") cake board from the top of both cakes. On one cake replace it with a 12.5cm (5") cake board, attached with a little chocolate ganache. Spread a little more ganache on top of the 12.5cm (5") board. Turn over the second cake and place the exposed top onto the 12.5cm (5") board on the first cake. Set aside for one hour to return to room temperature.

26 Spread more ganache around the whole double-barrel cake with a large palette knife (T) then use a large chocolate scraper to achieve a smooth finish (U).

27 Once the surface is as smooth as possible, heat the chocolate scraper under hot water. Dry it with kitchen paper then use the hot scraper to smooth the whole cake in one motion to give it a clean finish. Place the cake in the refrigerator for 20 minutes to set.

28 Warm the blade of a small, sharp knife in hot, boiled water then dry it with some kitchen paper. Use the hot knife to remove the uppermost cake board.

29 Spread some chocolate ganache on top of the cake with a palette knife until smooth. Heat an icing ruler or large palette knife under hot water, dry it with kitchen paper then scrape it across the top of the cake to achieve a smooth finish. Place the cake in the fridge for 20 minutes to set.

30 Use a hot, sharp knife to carefully remove any excess chocolate from the top edge of the cake and create a smooth edge.

DECORATION

31 Cut out five 48cm (19") long strips of acetate with 1–3cm (3/8–1 1/8") widths.

32 Mix the purple dust food colour into the tempered white chocolate. Transfer both this and the tempered dark chocolate into large piping bags.

33 Lay two of the strips on the work surface and snip off the end of the bag of purple chocolate. Pipe a line of chocolate along each strip (V). Use a palette knife to spread it into an even, thin layer which reaches over the edges of the acetate (W).

34 Working with one at a time, pick up each strip of acetate from one end (X) and run your fingers down both edges to smooth them (Y). Place it on a clean area of work surface at room temperature and leave it for three to five minutes or as soon as it has a matt surface.

35 Pipe a little more chocolate down the centre of the strip. Wrap the acetate sheet around the cake with the chocolate facing inwards, with an overlap at the back.

36 Repeat steps 33–35 with the dark chocolate and the remaining three acetate strips. Place the cake in the refrigerator for approximately 30 minutes.

37 Peel away the acetate strips one by one, being careful where they overlap. Some chocolate will come away with the section that overlaps. Finish with some fresh, food-safe flowers just before serving.

38 Store the cake in a cool, dry place away from strong odours for up to four days. It's best not to store it in the refrigerator as water droplets will form on the surface.

TROPICAL SUNSHINE
WEDDING CAKE

This design will bring a burst of sunshine to any celebration. Ganache is whipped into a light, fluffy and mousse-like consistency before filling the cake, and juicy mango works beautifully with the smooth milk and white chocolates in this recipe.

INGREDIENTS

Chocolate Glaze

12 sheets of leaf gelatine

300g (10½oz) liquid glucose

300g (10½oz) caster sugar

200g (7oz) condensed milk

300g (10½) white chocolate, chopped or in callets

Dust food colours: 2tsp Red and 4tsp Yellow (SK)

Mango Ganache Mousse and Fresh Mango Filling

Round cake size	10cm (4")	15cm (6")	20.5cm (8")	25.5cm (10")
Mango purée	115g (4oz)	225g (8oz)	335g (11¾oz)	560g (1lb 3¾oz)
Whipping cream	30ml (1fl oz)	60ml (2fl oz)	90ml (3fl oz)	150ml (5¼fl oz)
Milk chocolate, chopped or in callets	300g (10½oz)	600g (1lb 5¼oz)	900g (2lb)	1.5kg (3lb 5oz)
Fresh mango, cut into small dice	80g (2¾oz)	160g (5½oz)	240g (8½oz)	400g (14oz)

Chocolate Sponge

Round cake size	10cm (4")	15cm (6")	20.5cm (8")	25.5cm (10")
Ground almonds	95g (3¼oz)	185g (6½oz)	280g (9¾oz)	460g (1lb¼oz)
Caster sugar (first quantity)	105g (3¾oz)	215g (7¾oz)	320g (11¼oz)	540oz (1lb 3oz)
Plain flour	15g (½oz)	30g (1oz)	45g (1½oz)	75g (2½oz)
Cocoa powder	8g (¼oz)	15g (½oz)	20g (¾oz)	35g (1¼oz)
Unsalted butter, melted	20g (¾oz)	35g (1¼oz)	55g (2oz)	90g (3oz)
Large eggs, whole	1	2	3	5
Large eggs, separated	2	4	6	10
Caster sugar (second quantity; for the egg whites)	15g (½oz)	30g (1oz)	45g (1½oz)	75g (2½oz)
Salt	Small pinch	Pinch	Large pinch	2 pinches
Baking trays	1	2	3	5
No. of strips	4	8	12	20
Cake boards	2 x 10cm (4")	2 x 15cm (6")	2 x 20.5cm (8")	2 x 25.5cm (10")

Covering

Round cake size	10cm (4")	15cm (6")	20.5cm (8")	25.5cm (10")
White chocolate modelling paste (SK)	400g (14oz)	800g (1lb 12oz)	1kg (2lb 3¼oz)	1.4kg (3lb 1½oz)
Size of strip	34cm x 9.5cm (13³/₈" x 3¾")	50cm x 9.5cm (19⁵/₈" x 3¾")	65cm x 9.5cm (25½" x 3¾")	82cm x 9.5cm (32" x 3¾")

Chocolate Flower

300g (10½oz) white chocolate, tempered

Red dust food colour (SK)

EQUIPMENT

Basic equipment (see page 18)

30cm x 38cm (12" x 15") flat baking tray(s)

8cm x 28cm (3¹/₈" x 11") rectangular food-grade card template

Cake dowels (for tiered cakes only)

Half-sphere, multiple-cavity polycarbonate chocolate moulds: 4cm, 2 x 5cm, 6cm and 7cm (1½", 2 x 2", 2³/₈" and 2¾")

Cake smoothers

MAKES 67 DESSERT PORTIONS OR 134 COFFEE PORTIONS

CHOCOLATE GLAZE

1 Soak the gelatine in a small bowl with 120ml (4¼fl oz) of water for 10 minutes.

2 Heat the liquid glucose, caster sugar, condensed milk and 150ml (5¼fl oz) of water in a large saucepan until it reaches 103°C (217°F). Remove from the heat and allow to cool slightly.

3 Add the soaked gelatine and its water to the warm mixture, blending with a stick blender until fully combined. Add the white chocolate and blend again until melted and fully combined.

4 Place three quarters of the mixture in one bowl and the other quarter in another. Colour the larger amount yellow and the smaller amount red by adding dust food colours and blending until the colour is even.

5 Pour each glaze through a sieve into a jug. Cover with cling film against the surface of the glaze and leave to cool to room temperature. Place in the refrigerator overnight to rest.

MANGO GANACHE MOUSSE

TOP TIP

If you can't find mango purée then blend strained, tinned mango instead and use the equivalent total weight of the ingredients. Add some of the juice if necessary.

6 Heat the cream and mango purée to just before boiling and allow to cool to 38°C (100°F).

7   Heat the chocolate gently in a microwave or bain-marie. Remove from the heat before it has fully melted, when it reaches 32°C (90°F).

8   When both are the correct temperature, pour the mango cream into the chocolate (A) and use a stick blender to blend until fully incorporated (B).

9   Cover with cling film against the surface of the ganache and leave to cool to room temperature. Place in the refrigerator overnight to rest.

CHOCOLATE SPONGE

10   Preheat the oven to 200°C (400°F/gas mark 6). Grease the baking trays with a light coating of oil then line them with silicone baking mats (silicone baking mats are best for this recipe as the sponge can ripple while it's baking).

11   Beat together the almonds, the first quantity of caster sugar, flour, cocoa powder, melted butter, whole eggs and egg yolks at a medium speed for five minutes.

12   In a clean bowl, whisk the egg whites, second quantity of caster sugar and salt until the mixture forms firm peaks.

13   Beat a third of the whisked egg whites into the almond mixture until fully combined, then gradually and carefully fold in the rest of the whites with a spatula.

TOP TIP

It's important not to over-mix when adding the egg whites as you'll lose air and therefore volume. The mixture could become too runny, making the sponge strips thinner and more likely to burn.

14   Spread the mixture over the lined baking trays, right up to the edges. Bake the sponges for 10–15 minutes or until they start to turn golden brown around the edges. Remove the trays from the oven and leave the sponges to stand for three minutes.

15   Turn the first sponge onto a sheet of greaseproof paper and peel off the backing paper very carefully. Lay the backing paper back on top of the sponge and turn the next sponge onto it. Peel off and replace the backing paper as before, and continue to stack the sponges in this way. Leave the cakes to cool for 20 minutes; they should not cool completely in this time.

16   Remove the sponges from the greaseproof paper and use the 8cm x 28cm (3^1/$_8$" x 11") rectangular template to cut out four strips from each sponge (C). Return the sponge pieces to the greaseproof paper and leave them to cool completely.

ASSEMBLY

17   Beat the ganache in a stand mixer fitted with the paddle attachment until light, fluffy and mousse-like. Transfer the ganache mousse to a large piping bag, snip off the end and pipe it onto one of the sponge strips (D). Use a palette knife to spread the ganache mousse into a 4–5mm (^{3}/$_{16}$–^{1}/$_4$") thick layer (E). Sprinkle some fresh mango over the top (F). Use a palette knife to press the mango down into the ganache mousse (G).

TOP TIP

It's best to used diced, fresh mango as tinned fruit would be too soggy to fill the cake.

18   Starting from the short end (H), roll up the sponge tightly with the mousse on the inside (I).

19   Repeat step 17 to cover the next sponge sheet with a layer of ganache mousse and mango. Attach the sheet to the sponge cylinder where the first strip finishes (J) and continue to roll it up (K).

20   Place the sponge cylinder in the centre of the cake board and repeat step 19 to continue adding sponge strips to the central roll until it reaches the edge of the cake board.

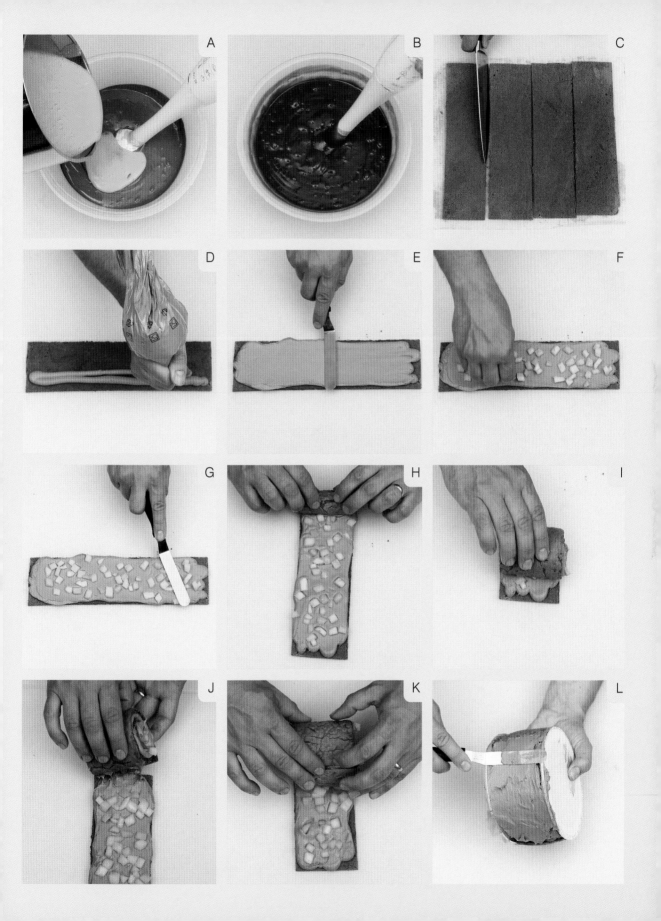

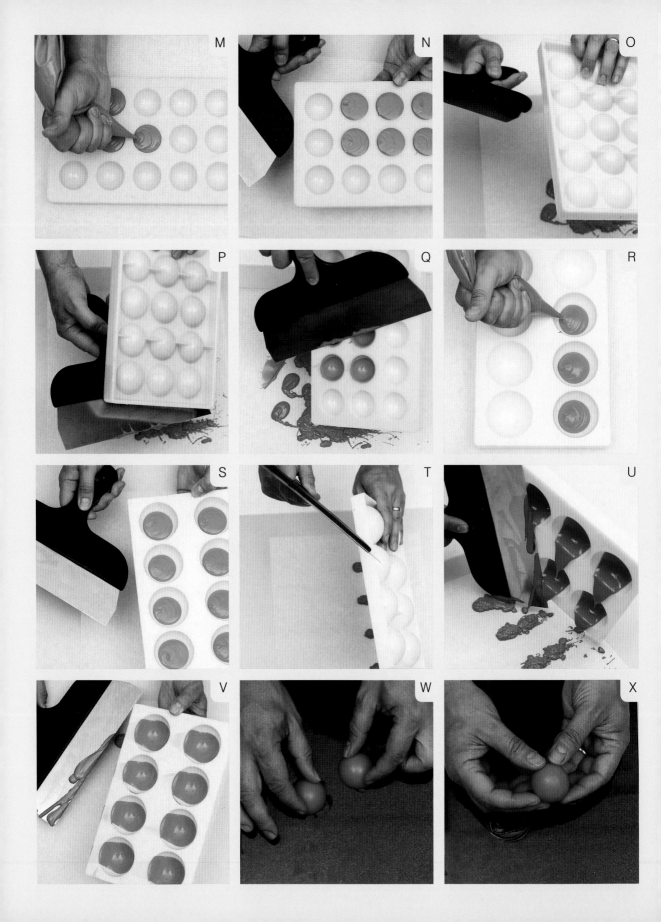

21   Place another cake board of the same size upside down on top of the cake. Use the two boards as a guide to spread a layer of ganache mousse around the side of the cake with a palette knife (L, see page 183). Remove the top board and cover the top of the cake with ganache mousse. Place the cake in the refrigerator for one hour to set.

22   Roll out a quarter of the white chocolate modelling paste to a 4mm (³/₁₆") thickness and cut around a cake board the same size as the cake to make a disc. Place the disc on top of the cake.

23   Roll the remaining chocolate modelling paste into a long sausage. Roll out the sausage to a 4mm (³/₁₆") thickness and use a sharp knife to cut out the strip: the width should be the same as the height of the cake and the length should be the circumference. There's a guide to these measurements in the table at the beginning of this recipe on page 181.

24   Wrap the strip around the side of the cake and trim the end to make a neat join. Use cake smoothers to create a smooth, crisp finish. Place the cake in the freezer for one to two hours.

TOP TIP

If you are making a tiered cake, dowel the tiers before placing them in the freezer. Stack the cakes before glazing them all in one go to create the smoothest possible finish.

CHOCOLATE FLOWER

25   Make sure the moulds are clean and free from grease and water. Colour the tempered white chocolate by mixing in the red dust food colour. Transfer the coloured chocolate to a large piping bag and snip off the end.

26   Pipe the chocolate into six cavities of the 4cm (1½") mould as quickly as you can (M). Use a scraper to scrape the excess chocolate from the top of the mould if necessary. Tap the mould with the side of the scraper to release any air bubbles from the surface of the mould (N).

27   Turn the mould upside down to release the excess chocolate. Tap the side of the mould with a scraper, keeping the mould level at all times (O). Once the chocolate has stopped dripping, scrape the mould again, this time whilst it is upside down, so the excess chocolate falls out of the mould (P).

28   Turn the mould the right way up and clean it with a scraper again (Q). Place the mould upside down on a piece of silicone paper until the chocolate is touch-dry, then place in the refrigerator to fully set for no more than 30 minutes.

29   Pipe chocolate into all eight wells of the 5cm (2") mould, this time filling only the very bottom of the well (R). Tap the mould with the side of the scraper to release any air bubbles from the surface of the mould (S).

30   Turn the mould on its side to release the excess chocolate. Tap the side of the mould with a scraper, keeping the mould level at all times (T). Once the chocolate has stopped dripping, scrape the mould again, still while it's on its side, to remove the excess chocolate (U). Repeat step 28 (V).

31   Repeat steps 29–30 with the 5cm, 6cm and 7cm (2", 2 ³/₈" and 2¾") moulds.

32   Heat a granite slab or metal baking tray in the oven on a low heat for 10 minutes. Scoop the chocolate half-spheres out of the moulds.

33   Remove the slab from the oven and place it on a heatproof work surface. Take a 4cm (1½") half-sphere in each hand and briefly place the open edge onto the hot surface (W), then immediately stick them together (X). Clean away any excess chocolate around the join with your fingertip if necessary.

34   Place the domed side of a third 4cm (1½") half-sphere onto the hot surface until it melts a 2cm (¾") hole in the top (Y, see overleaf). Immediately place the whole sphere on top of the hole (Z) and join them together using a little freeze spray. If you'd like to make it stronger, pipe a little more chocolate around the join.

35 Remove all of the petals from the moulds: push the base down into the mould to scoop them out. Place them in groups of the same sizes. Temper the remaining red chocolate, fill a small paper piping bag and snip off the end.

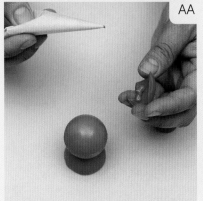

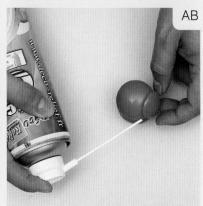

36 Pipe a little tempered red chocolate onto the base of a 5cm (2") petal (AA) and attach it to the side of the sphere, leaving a small gap between the top of the petal and the sphere. Secure the join with a little freeze spray (AB).

37 Continue to add petals in the same way, overlapping them slightly (AC, AD); you should fit five or six petals onto this first layer.

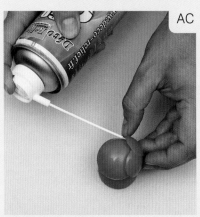

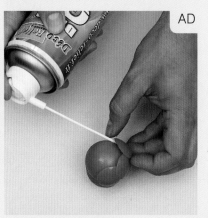

38 Add another layer of six or seven 5cm (2") petals, followed by seven 6cm (2²/₈") petals and seven 7cm (2¾") petals, opening them out a little more each time.

TOP TIP

If you don't have all of the half-sphere moulds, you could make this flower with just the 4cm (1½") mould for the spheres and the 5cm (2") mould for the petals.

GLAZING THE CAKE

39 On the day you plan to serve the cake, heat the glaze to 30–35°C (86–95°F) in a microwave or over a bain-marie.

TROPICAL SUNSHINE WEDDING CAKE

40 Remove the cake from the freezer and place it on a wire rack over a large, rimmed tray. Pour the yellow glaze over the cake all in one go (AE–AJ). There will be a lot of glaze but this is necessary in order to achieve a smooth, even coverage. Once the entire cake is covered, pour the red glaze down one side: stop pouring when it reaches the third tier and it should flow down the remaining tiers (AK–AN).

TOP TIP

It's a good idea to practise pouring the glaze over a different cake or cake dummy before attempting it on the real cake. As the glaze needs to be poured all in one go, there is only one chance to get it right. You can gather the glaze from the clean tray and reheat it before using it on the real cake.

41 Wait for the glaze to stop dripping from the bottom edge of the cake then use a large, slightly wet palette knife to lift the cake off the rack. Rotate the cake carefully and use the palette knife to remove the excess glaze from the base of the cake. While the glaze is still wet, add the chocolate flower. Leave the cake to set for at least one hour in a cool, dry place – or in the refrigerator if it's a hot day – before serving.

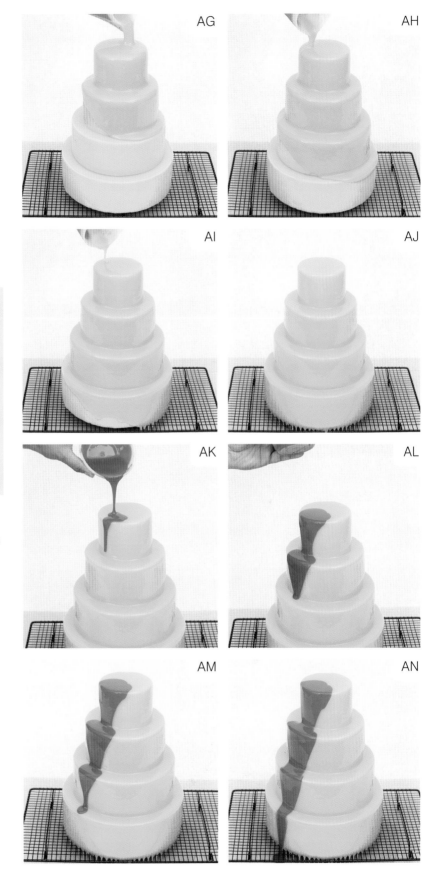

AG AH AI AJ AK AL AM AN

INDEX

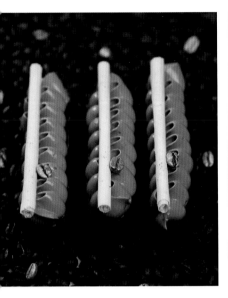

Squires Kitchen, UK
Squires House
3 Waverley Lane
Farnham
Surrey
GU9 8BB
+44 (0)1252 260 260
squires-shop.com

Squires Kitchen International School, UK
The Grange
Hones Yard
Farnham
Surrey
GU9 8BB
+44 (0)1252 260 262
squires-school.co.uk

OTHER BOOKS BY MARK TILLING

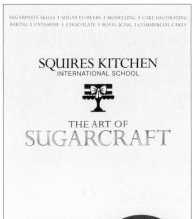

B. Dutton Publishing is an award-winning
publisher of cake decorating, chocolate and sugarcraft titles.
To find out more about our books, follow us at
facebook.com/bduttonpublishing and twitter.com/bduttonbooks.